12 - 14 -12

Emily –
    I can't tell you how much
it meant to me that you
were the first student to
read this ... not to mention
how much I value the
feedback you gave me.
Keep fighting the good fight!

W. B.

Compelled: A Memoir of OCD, Anxiety, Depression, Bi-Polar Disorder, and Faith…Sometimes

By: Tim Blue

BY THE SAME AUTHOR

Mentor-Teaching in the English Classroom

Cover image by Julie Rodriguez

Cover image rights purchased at Fotosearch.com (K2416421)
Standard License

ISBN-13: 978-0615737904 (Timothy R. Blue)

ISBN-10: 0615737900

For Annie

"If you think anyone is sane you just don't know enough about them."

-Christopher Moore, *Practical Demonkeeping*

Chapter 1: How Did I End Up Here?

"I need you to remove the shoelaces from your shoes," the woman said to me.

"Why do you need my shoelaces?" I asked.

"We have to take anything away from you that you could use to harm yourself," she replied.

"I think there's been a mistake," I said, shivering both from the cold and from fear. "The intake woman told me I was coming here as a 'voluntary' patient and that I would be able to leave of my own accord. I don't want to kill myself or I wouldn't be here. That's the whole reason I went to the ER in the first place – because I wanted to jump in front of a bus. But I knew my pregnant wife and daughter would not appreciate my doing that. I don't think this is the place I thought it was. Can I please just go home?"

"You can request to leave, but the doctor doesn't have to release you for 72 hours," she said calmly, almost coldly. This woman – an intake nurse at the psychiatric hospital where I had landed after a bout of suicidal depression – had had this conversation before, and she had memorized the answers. I was just another patient. Not Tim Blue, English teacher at a respected private school, graduate of Wake Forest University, Ph.D. from Georgia State University, son of a well-known Christian author and speaker, member of a family that "has it all together."

Starting to panic I said, "Well, when can I see my family again? I need them to help me get through this. I wouldn't have agreed to come here if I knew I would be this trapped."

"Visiting hours are for one hour twice a week. The next hours are tomorrow night from 6-7. You can't have visitors any more often than that."

One hour twice a week? I was trapped, literally locked in.

The men's ward wasn't the sort of place that cheered one up. It seemed more like a place that would instigate suicide than one that would keep me from it. I was stuck for at least three days in a poorly lit, dingy hell hole, at the mercy of a psychiatrist I hadn't even met, at the mercy of these nurses who didn't know my story, who didn't know that I wasn't like these other men. I was very sane actually. I was "normal" for the most part (or so I thought at the time). I was just having an episode, and I was fairly sure it was a reaction to Luvox, my latest anti-depressant, not some fundamental flaw inside my brain that made me feel like the lights had gone out in the universe, like taking the next step was torture, like crying for absolutely no reason at all for hours at a time, like getting hit by an 18-wheeler would be the essence of bliss.

"Let me repeat," I felt like yelling, "I am NORMAL. Let me out of here!"

My sister had told me about a recent book she'd read wherein a lady experienced a severe bout of depression. All the lady could think to do was to recite, "The Lord is my Shepherd" over and over again. What could it hurt? I tried it:

"TheLordismyShepherd. TheLordismyShepherd. TheLordismyShepherd. TheLordismyShepherd. TheLordismyShepherd. TheLordismyShepherd. TheLordismyShepherd," I said, trying to quell the rising panic.

Nothing. Perhaps God didn't want to come to the mental hospital either. Maybe I was as on my own spiritually as I felt, as I feared.

TheLordismyShepherd. TheLordismyShepherd. TheLordismyShepherd. TheLordismyShepherd. TheLordismyShepherd. TheLordismyShepherd. TheLordismyShepherd. TheLordismyShepherd.

Still nothing.

***

I wish this was the part of the story where I woke up from the dream. But it wasn't a dream. It was real. In the fall of 2009, I spent three days in a psychiatric hospital. I was locked behind a metal door with thirty-some-odd complete strangers who, for all I knew, were the type of people one often associates with a mental hospital – people who drool and think they are Abraham Lincoln. People who plan to marry the Little Mermaid. Crazy people.

The only outside space we were allowed to visit was paved with concrete, about 10 feet by 10 feet, and it had barbed wire at the top of it. Since nearly everyone smoked, there was no way to even get fresh air for the 30 minutes a day I was allowed outside. Inside was worse. Men sat in the common area looking blankly off into space. I tried to strike up conversation with a few, thought if I could make a friend I might feel less panicked, but most of them weren't interested in talking. Many of them were used to places like this – regulars, if you will. One man even offered me a detailed comparison between this hospital and the other primary psychiatric hospital in the area. He liked the other one better.

***

After my conversation with the woman who told me I was stuck here for at least 3 days, I was led to my room by a large black man, one of the interns. He asked me to strip all the way down to my underwear. Eventually, I had to pull down my pants just to prove that I didn't have a knife between my butt cheeks or a grenade hanging from my penis. I didn't have either, so he let me pull my pants back up.

While I stood there shivering uncontrollably from both fear and cold, he told me a million things I already knew: how I needed to find a good therapist, one I really trusted; how I needed to get on the right medication; how I needed to stay off drugs and alcohol as they could contribute to my mental health problems; and finally, how I didn't seem like their normal clientele.

"Uh, yeah, I've been trying to tell you people that there's been a mistake! I am NORMAL. I have a job, a wife, a daughter, a child on the way, a mortgage, and a dog. I don't belong here." But the orderlies in mental hospitals are used to "crazy" people telling them all sorts of lies. Everything out of my mouth was met with a condescending grin. I thought they might even reach out and pat me on the head like a puppy if I got close enough. "There, there, now," they all seemed to think, "I'm sure you're very normal, but run along with the others, and we'll let the doctors know just how normal you think you are."

Later that evening, this same man gave a remarkably lengthy talk to us about what Heroin does to one's brain. "Heroin?!" I thought. "He's telling us why Heroin is bad. I've never even smoked a cigarette. I've never even been in the same room as someone who was smoking pot. I didn't get drunk for the first time until I was in my mid-twenties. Heroin?! What kind of people am I in here with?!"

Turns out, "those people" were some of the kindest and sanest people I've ever met, but more on that at a later time. For now, I was convinced that I was living in an alternate reality, a wretched nightmare. Maybe I was indeed having a bad drug trip as we spoke, and I was just imagining the clean-cut, naïve guy I thought I was.

***

In the days that followed, some of the longest and slowest of my life, my own sanity returned as Luvox made its way out of my system. I had been put on Luvox, the first line of defense to battle OCD chemically, by a(nother) new psychiatrist. Within a few days of starting it, I felt profoundly depressed, something I was not familiar with at the time, though unfortunately I have become good friends with it recently. I had always been anxious and obsessive, but generally positive and optimistic on the whole. After starting Luvox, something wasn't right. I felt like I was floating in outer space, far away from reality. I also felt deep anger and darkness washing over my brain. After "forging ahead because I was finally going to trust this psychiatrist" for a few days, I called the psychiatrist one night, despondent. He wanted me to come see him the next day, so I did. That particular day had been pretty good, largely, I think, because I knew I was going to see him later that day, and I was sure he'd know how to fix this new problem. My mistake was in telling him I had had a good day, so he thought I had turned a corner because of the medication. "Let's go ahead and go up on your dosage from 100 to 150 mg – the full recommended dosage," he said.

"Are you sure it's not the medicine causing me to feel this way? Are you sure I won't feel worse?" I pleaded, terrified at his suggestion given that I felt as disconnected from my normal reality as if I had woken up as a giant bug, like the man in "The Metamorphosis," by Franz Kafka.

"It's not the medicine. You're just depressed," he said. "We need to get you up to a higher dose."

"Okay, I'll do what you say." I had been a bad patient up to this point, taking myself on and off of medications without the previous psychiatrists' go-ahead. I had doubted their diagnoses. I was determined to see my medication therapy through this time.

I went up on the dose, and within a few days, I felt literally incapable of seeing the good in the world. There's no other way to describe it other than to say that the lights had gone out in the universe. The hope I had clung to throughout my life rang hollow. I was suicidal.

When I got ahold of this doctor on a Friday night around 10 p.m., I told him in no uncertain terms I was 100% sure the medicine was making me deeply, deeply depressed. He reluctantly said I could go off of it, still convinced that I needed to let it do its job for more than the ten days I had given it. I asked if I needed to wean myself. He said, "No, you haven't been on it long enough to need to wean off of it. Just stop the medication." Boy was he wrong.

The next day, a Saturday, I felt more hopeful, but a strong sense of sadness. It seemed like it had to do with meds, but according to the psychiatrist, I wouldn't have withdrawal effects. By Sunday afternoon, I collapsed on the bed and cried for twenty minutes for absolutely no reason. On Monday morning, I fell to the floor of my closet in deep despair and sadness, crying again. I stayed home from work and spent the day clinging to my wife's side because I was so scared to be alone. On Tuesday, I forced myself to head to work again, but after a couple of hours, I left right in the middle of the day. I called a fellow teacher, who happened to be one of my closest friends, and told him I had class in five minutes and he would have to cover for me. I couldn't even hold back the tears until I got to the car. I was walking through my school's campus sobbing. My friend asked me if I was heading to a safe place. He knew I was suicidal.

***

I made it home from school without succumbing to the urge to turn into oncoming traffic. Thankfully, my wife was there. Had she not been, I might well not have survived that day. She wasn't supposed to be there at that time, but her plans had changed at the last minute. I'm not going to say, "God ordained that she was there" because a lot of people kill themselves and God doesn't seem to show up for them. I don't know if God caused her to be there or not, but I'm certainly grateful that she was.

A few hours later, I lay shivering on the couch, unable to get warm. I told my wife and parents, who had come over to offer their support, that I needed to be in the hospital. We decided against going to the psychiatric hospital and opted for the ordinary ER instead, hoping they could give me some sort of drug to counteract the medication reaction I was having.

By that night, I was in the psychiatric hospital. The normal-people ER weren't easily fooled. They shipped me straight over.

***

The following day, I met my new psychiatrist, a short, Indian man named Dr. Dutta. By the time I got to him, I had seen my other psychiatrist multiple times, my primary care physician, and the emergency room doctor. To a person, they all told me that there was little to no chance I was having a reaction to the medication. They were dismissive, even cold – told me I was depressed and needed to trust their judgment as well as the medication. Had any one of them told me what Dr. Dutta told me, I might well have been able to hold out for another day or two without submitting to the trauma of the psych ward.

Dr. Dutta told me he had seen a million cases like mine – type "A" people who are riddled with anxiety and end up having a breakdown of some sort. He told me what I had suspected was the truth – I was "normal," and I would be just fine in a few days. His calm demeanor and kind words gave me hope. He put me on some sleeping meds and some sort of anti-anxiety medication that got me through the next few psych-ward-trapped, anxiety-filled days. The depression subsided gradually, and the lights in the universe came back on little by little.

***

After my own bout with suicidal thoughts, I will never again offer the common refrain regarding suicide – that it's "selfish." Suicide is despair in action – true despair personified. No one who has some hope left kills himself. I was incapable of seeing the good side of anything – my yet-to-be-born child; my two-year-old daughter's new words and abilities; my parents and siblings who loved me; my just-beginning career, teaching a subject I was passionate about. Having stood at the brink of suicide, I can say with certainty that, while it might technically be selfish, the person who commits the act has no other option.

I think there were two things that kept me from acting on my impulse to kill myself: 1. My obligations to my family, but frankly, those only offered short-term hope. I knew that if I didn't feel better, that rationale wouldn't help for long. 2. My fear of hell. From childhood, I had been implanted with the idea that suicide might well be an unforgivable sin, and I had been told in no uncertain terms that hell was an all-too-real place of eternal torture with no way out. So it was possible, then, that killing myself might not actually bring relief but additional pain and torture. (Much more on hell in the appendix as I know it is a central issue for religious people struggling with OCD. Just Google "religious OCD" or "scrupulosity" and see for yourself.) If God wouldn't come through and help me overcome my mental struggles, I might well be completely, utterly screwed – damned either to a life of misery or to an eternity of even worse misery. I was left without a good option, so I eventually chose the mental hospital as plan C.

***

I left the hospital after three days. My wife came to pick me up, and I have never felt freer than that day. In fact, the next few days were some of the best of my life. It's remarkable how calm an obsessive-compulsive brain can be when it thinks it has finally faced the hell he has always feared. "You made it through that," I thought, "and now everything will be fine."

Everything was fine, and for maybe the millionth time in my life, I thought I had finally fixed that broken part of my brain. This lasted for about a week. Then my normal brain chemistry took over again, the old fears crept to life, and I was back where I started – just me, my faith in a God who supposedly loved me, and OCD.

Chapter 2: The Beginning of the End(less Doubts and Fears)

My parents have told me that my compulsive tendencies started with I was a very small child. Apparently, I began rubbing my fingers raw with anxiety even before I can remember. I still do. I had nightmares from which I would wake up screaming bloody murder earlier than I can even remember (my mom tells me). But I'll begin when I became aware of the mental battle that has characterized my existence.

Sometime around that vague time in life when I had my earliest memory, I became afraid that my parents would abandon me – just drop me off someplace and never come back. Other than the fact that they had four other kids to tend to and might well be looking to get rid of the most high-maintenance one, I had no reason to believe that this would be the case. Still, as the time approached at which they were supposed to pick me up from school, baseball, a friend's house or anywhere else, I would begin to compulsively check the clock and look out whatever window was available.

I'd think: "Where are they? Why aren't they here yet? This is it; they've finally decided to just up and ditch me. I knew it I knew it I knew it! Where are they? Why aren't they here yet? Wouldn't a parent who cared about her children be at least fifteen minutes early? I see other moms lining up already. I knew this would happen. She won't come for me. All the other parents and teachers and administrators will give me a patronizing smile as they watch me suffer with loneliness. Meanwhile, they'll get in their cars and drive away until I am ALONE. Where will I sleep? Will some mass murderer come for me once it turns dark? I'm sure he will! Now there's only fourteen minutes until she's supposed to be here and there are at least four or five moms already here. I'm done for. Abandoned."

When my mom finally came around the corner and into my vision, waves of relief washed over me. Salvation! Everything would be fine. She did still love me! My parents probably had a long talk about whether or not to pick me up today or to go ahead and jump ship on me. Mercifully, at least for today, they decided to show up. Phew! I'll never have to worry again.

Until tomorrow.

***

The first tangible memory of this obsessive fear controlling my life is inextricably intertwined with my religious upbringing. And to this day, the two primary influences on my cognitive life have been OCD and Christianity.

It was on a gray fall Sunday at First Baptist Church in downtown Atlanta. The fear was extra-bad that day. Anyone with any persistent ailment will understand that some days are just way worse than others.

I nearly had a panic attack as I walked through the classroom doors and away from my parents. I felt trapped and terrified, almost out of my own body, as I would feel decades later when I ended up in the hospital. I made it through the socializing time without actually breaking down into tears. But when the time for juice and cookies arrived, I was on the brink of falling apart.

I was fighting mightily to maintain composure and dignity, my greatest fear (to this day) being embarrassment. "Hold it together, hold it together, hold it together, and don't be a sissy, Tim," I repeated, looking for a way out of my imminent collapse and humiliation.

I laid my head down on the table, looking for a way to mask the oncoming tears. The teacher dutifully caught my cue and asked if I was okay.

"I don't feel good," I responded, trying to make my face look like someone who was about to throw up.

"Do you need me to take you to the bathroom?"

This wasn't what I was hoping for. I wanted my parents, not the bathroom, so I stalled: "No, I guess not." I kept my head on that table, though, hoping my prolonged, feigned misery might eventually spark a different line of conversation.

Eventually, I put on a strong enough performance that he asked if I needed him to take me to my parents. "Um, I guess that's a good idea," I said, not wanting to sound too eager despite being as eager as a virgin on his wedding night.

The teacher took me to find my parents at the nearby Hardee's, where they would go for some much deserved time to themselves while the five of us kids were being babysat for free in Sunday School. The mental relief as we headed out the door of the classroom, knowing that we were heading toward my short-term salvation, was palpable.

When I walked through the door of that Hardee's, I felt overwhelming shame. My assumption was that they were thinking something along these lines: "What are we going to do with this kid? How can he not get it through his head that we won't leave him? Isn't he a little too old to be like this?" After all, this would be what I would think if I were in their shoes.

As much as I had tried to hide my fear out of intense shame, they *knew*, and I knew that they knew what was really going on. They knew I wasn't sick, though they were kind enough not to tell my teacher to take me back to class. They knew that that morning the OCD had been particularly bad. They knew that the additional fifty questions (up from the normal twenty or thirty) about when and where they were going to pick me up meant I was feeling particularly ill-at-ease. And at that moment, I knew something, too – I knew that I would need to develop a better coping mechanism for hiding my ever-present fear. I would need to find new ways to manipulate reassurance out of them (and others) that didn't betray my wimpiness or my lack of faith in my parents. I didn't want to keep feeling obsessed about abandonment, but I didn't want to keep experiencing the shame I felt in that Hardee's either. What to do?!

***

This dichotomy of feelings has plagued me ever since that moment. I have spent much of my life trying to manipulate reassurance out of people. Tormented by irrational fears…fears that I am well aware are irrational…fears of rogue germs, lost salvation, damnation to hell, parental abandonment, accidentally offending someone and creating a catastrophe…If I admitted to my average friend that I was internally freaking out about some off-handed comment they had just made which caused me to question the security of our relationship, I would look like a freak. So I would have to manipulate the conversation back around to what they said so I could get reassurance that I misheard them. Or I would be going insane about the fact that I touched the handle to the bathroom door with my bare hands, and I would find a way to "casually" bring up the issue of germs to the adult nearby, seeking his/her wisdom about the science of catching AIDS or cancer.

I'm sure these childhood conversations were never as skillful as I thought, but I can tell you that years of practice has made me an adult that hides my obsessions very well. Countless people over the years have been shocked when I reveal my inner anxiety to them. I hide it behind a façade of put-togetherness. I wear nice clothes, come from a respected family, groom myself well, have multiple degrees, have a "perfect" little family of my own. But it's a costume. I'm certifiably crazy on the inside.

***

After this talk with my parents at Hardee's, I had my first experience with the blissful feeling of relief that comes when one thinks the Biggest Problem in life has been solved. I thought, "That reassuring conversation was all I needed – a good sit-down chat with mom and dad to know that they really, really promise not to leave me somewhere by myself. Phew. All. Better." At least once every few months, I get this same sensation. Sometimes it lasts an hour; sometimes a few weeks. But it never, ever lasts. Ever.

***

My next tangible memory came after school one day when I was in 2nd or 3rd grade. The fear was really bad that day, too. I drilled my mom on the specifics of the time and place of her return to pick me up: 3:00. Sidewalk outside the gym.

I arrived at that precise spot at 3:00:32, thirty-two seconds after school had let out and thirty-two seconds after my mom had promised to be parked right in that particular spot. She wasn't there.

My mom had been unable to park in the precise spot I had asked her to, and she had pulled around the corner, no more than fifty feet away. She sent my sister back in search of me.

When my sister came around the corner looking to tell me where she was parked, I tried to hide the tears, knowing I was acting crazy. Whether or not she actually saw the tears was beside the point in my mind. If there was even a slight chance she had, I needed to save face in case she had seen I was upset (well, not just upset actually – more like convinced that I was on my own at age eight. Left. Abandoned. A.L.O.N.E. So, yeah, pretty upset). But I hid it – blinked the tears away and sniffed the runny nose away while walking to the car, cool as a cucumber, just a kid getting picked up for carpool. Nothing to see here, people! Don't worry about me.

But here was another taste of that crippling shame that who I really was needed to be put in a closet, hidden as far from human eyes as possible. "Don't be such a sissy, Tim. Quit acting like a baby. You're eight freakin' years old. Grow up already."

***

A year later, I quit little league baseball because of my OCD – something I will forever regret because I still believe I was headed to play in the majors – probably short stop for the Atlanta Braves with a career batting average around .400.

I had played for a number of years, and if I do say so myself, I had a lot of promise. A few major league scouts even came to my tee ball games from time to time. But attending practice was a nightmare because of the fact that my parents would usually drop me off for an hour with a group of strangers – my teammates and coach.

I remember the practice when it all came to a head – another one of those especially bad days. Practice was at a new place this time, and I remember it vividly: The field was tucked away down in a valley. Parents would drop their kids off at the top of a hill, and we had to trek down a steep incline for forty or fifty yards until it flattened out into a rather random set of fields.

Perhaps I am recalling it incorrectly, but I'm remembering what I felt, not what was real, keep in mind. To me it seemed like the worst possible place on earth for a kid with an obsessive fear of being abandoned to be forced to attend baseball practice. The field seemed like something out of a *Harry Potter* novel – a floating field of Purgatory. A perfect place to leave a kid because it was so secluded, so easy to make a getaway.

For some reason, my parents stayed up on the hill during practice. It must've had to do with me expressing terror to them, so I'm grateful that they stayed. But oh the shame I felt! I knew why they were there, and I knew they were at their wits' end with me.

Throughout practice, I tried to keep them in view. The field was angled so that, from my 2nd base post, I could glance up every ten seconds or so to make sure they hadn't escaped. I talked my coach into letting me show him how well I could bat left-handed because they would be visible from the left-handed batter's box. During team pow-wows, I pretended that the spots where my back would be to my parents weren't quite good enough, so I would round the circle until I could "listen to my coach" while keeping a close eye on my parents.

The ride home was one of *those* rides. Tense. In my eight or nine-year-old brain, I knew I needed to save face, to somehow convince them that all of my glances and checking didn't mean what they knew it meant. They tried to tell me once again that they weren't going to leave, but of course, their logic did me no good. This wasn't about logic. This was about brain chemistry gone awry and a little kid trying to save face with the people he most desperately wanted to please, to satisfy, to keep happy…so they wouldn't do what he feared most – jump ship on him.

They tried to reassure me.

I tried to believe them.

But I *couldn't*.

***

When sign-up time for the next season rolled around, I lied to them about why I thought it was time to hang up my glove. I told them I had lost interest. I put on my most nonchalant façade and told them I was bored with baseball, ready to pick a new sport in which to demonstrate my athletic prowess to the world. I wasn't sure what sport that would be just yet (but if it involved practices where they were going to leave me with near-strangers, I don't think it would've been the sport for me). Maybe I'd pick it up again the next year, I told them. Just need a break, you know. Kids these days have too much on their plates. I need some time to reflect on what to do next, ya know.

Again, they *knew*. Or at least in my brain, they knew. And they were ashamed. Or maybe I was ashamed and I was projecting, but the result was the same – I would have to build a thicker façade, work harder to convince these people I wanted desperately to please that I was worth loving.

To their credit, they allowed me to quit. I went to my brother's games filled with mixed emotions. I wanted to play baseball. I loved baseball. I was good at baseball. I missed baseball. But the relief at not having to live through the torture chamber of baseball practice tasted far good enough to compensate for the bitterness at having quit something I really liked.

***

Another early memory of OCD happened during routine car rides. I saw this time with my mom as a chance to have all my fears assuaged. For some bizarre reason, she got sick of the following pattern:

Me: "Mommy, what if you and daddy died? Who would take care of us?"

Mom: "Honey, that's not very likely to happen, but you would be well taken care of, I promise."

Me: "But what if whoever-it-was-who-was-assigned-this-lovely-duty died too? Then what?"

Mom: "Tim, I promise that you will be taken care of. That's not going to happen."

Me: "But what if it does?"

Mom: "Tim, you can only ask three more 'what if' questions. Then we're done!"

"Crap," I thought. "Three more?! But I have 1,763,501,268 more! And I have to pick three! Impossible."

At the heart of all of these "what ifs" was the same thing that was at the heart of my fear of being left somewhere by my parents: fear of abject disaster that I somehow could've prevented, if only...

***

At night, when the normal childhood nighttime fears overtook my not-so-normal brain, I would express this fear to my parents. Trying to help, they tried two tactics – logic and faith, neither of which do much for a chemical imbalance. Their first response was usually the obvious one: "Nothing bad is going to happen; we'll be right down the hall all night. We promise!" Apparently they were unaware of fires, rogue kidnappers, monsters under the bed and/or in the closet, the potential overnight death of every single person I knew on earth, or my own potential death. Sure, mom and dad! Nothing's going to happen. Yeah right.

They tried the faith route: "And if you're scared, just recite 1 John 4:18: 'Perfect love casts out fear.'"

So, I would lie in my bed, staring wide-eyed at the ceiling, knowing that if I went to sleep the rest of the family would either leave me to fend for myself or some horrible killer would break in and kill everyone else except me. Had Elizabeth Smart been kidnapped when I was still a child, I never would've slept, that's for sure.

1 John 4:18 became my nighttime mantra and it remained so well into my teenage years, when these same fears persisted: "Perfect love casts out fear. Perfect love casts out fear. Perfect love casts out fear…" Eventually, I would go to sleep, but in my estimation, this verse wasn't quite working the proper magic: I was either not loved perfectly, not reciting the right version of the verse, possessed by the devil

and therefore incapable of receiving the supposed peace this verse was supposed to bring, or I had somehow failed to demonstrate my love for God fully enough, so he was keeping this peace from me. Never once did the verse do anything for me except perhaps distract me a tiny bit from my fear as I chanted my mantra.

***

Sometime around this period of time, I think the seeds got planted for the deeply-rooted cynicism I still hold towards those who blithely cite scripture as a magical answer to one's problems. My brain ALWAYS sees the other side of the picture. Sure, I didn't kill myself when I ended up in the hospital, and I could say that God was there for me. But where was he for the Christian father of a student at my school who killed himself, leaving her mother with three small children? Did this man fail to quote the right scriptures?

Sure one person claims God told them to "claim" a verse and so-and-so got healed from cancer, but what about the other 6,342,158 people who felt the same promise from God only to find that the cancer had spread and the loved one was soon to die. Or why was "The Lord is my Shepherd" so helpful to that other depressed woman my sister had read about when it was useless to me during my time in the psychiatric ward? Does that mean that God actually isn't my Shepherd? Does it mean I'm not quite saying the verse right? Perhaps it was the wrong translation I was using? The verse did me about as much good as citing scripture after tearing my ACL. The verse might be true, but it wasn't doing anything for my present state.

For me, all this "name-it-claim-it" theology did was demonstrate once again the immense letdown of what I call "magical Christianity." Jesus didn't offer people pat answers to their questions. He never quoted scripture and told them to just recite that verse when they were scared to death at night. He healed people; he challenged the religious big-wigs of his day; and he spoke in metaphors about how to experience the kingdom of God.

One doesn't need to speak in metaphors if things are simple. One speaks in metaphors because simplistic verses don't tell the whole story. If the kingdom of God was so easy to experience, we wouldn't have so many different denominations proclaiming that they have IT right; we wouldn't have so many religions all telling us how to get close to God; and we wouldn't need a seminary degree to become a minister. The kingdom of God is hard to grasp, especially for those of us who can "what if" ourselves to death.

Here's my suggestion for you the next time a friend is suffering and a Bible verse comes to your mind: Hug them; sit down and buy them a few beers; talk to them; and maybe somewhere down the road you can share that verse with them. But don't think it's a cure-all. It's not.

If you really must have a verse to share with your struggling friends, share this one: "In this world you will have trouble. But take heart! I have overcome the world" (John 16:33 NIV). At least then you're struggling friend can see that Jesus was realistic and honest about life in this world. We do immense damage to the causes of God when we quote Bible verses out of context as if they were meant for specific instances and people in the year 2013. Sure, some apply, but be careful. Telling a homeless person that they should quote, "The Lord is my Shepherd, I shall not be in want" is as useful as offering Advil to someone with cancer.

***

My childhood fear of abandonment lasted until I was a young adult – around the time when reason naturally convinced me that I wasn't likely to be left alone on the earth in some post-apocalyptic world. Not that reason always (or ever) trumps OCD, but sometime around middle school my brain decided on a new course of action to keep me terrified, one that would be a lot less simple to "reason" my way out of. One that had to do with my eternal destiny.

Chapter 3: Highway to Hell (a.k.a. Middle School)

At its core, OCD is a quest for certainty where certainty doesn't/can't exist. The person who washes his hands a million times wants certainty that the deadly germs are banished from his hands, but he can never be sure. The driver who fears she has accidentally hit a pedestrian re-drives the same route over and over, looking for absolute certainty that she didn't hit the innocent pedestrian, but there's no way to be absolutely certain that that odd color on the sidewalk isn't the blood of the child she just ran over who is now at the hospital or the morgue. Or the kid who is terrified he'll be abandoned by his parents…he can never ask enough questions or stand in just the right spot to check on their early arrival so as to be completely certain that they will always come back.

Uncertainty dooms the sufferer of OCD to his torture chamber.

For the religious person, uncertainty will, at some point, attack his quest for peace through faith. Let's face it: religion comes with plenty of uncertainty. Sooner or later, everyone on the quest to understand or know God will have to ask some difficult questions: Why does God allow bad things to happen to good people? Why does God allow so much suffering when he could simply zap the evil-doers? What does it mean to be saved? Unsaved? Is there such a thing as hell, and if so, how do I know that the sweet little old lady who used to live next door who wasn't very religious but who was the kindest person I ever knew isn't there? (See appendix for a fuller discussion of hell).

My inevitable questions about the black-and-white certainties of the Christian faith caused the struggle between my internal self and my external self to rage on. Spiritual questions plagued my brain from the time I was old enough to ponder such matters, but the stakes were high in my family, where failure to see things the Right Way was not acceptable. My family's certainty mixed with my inevitable lack of certainty created a struggle within me between intellectual honesty and family acceptance – a struggle that persists to this day.

One of the certainties of my upbringing that troubled my uncertain brain was the question of hell. To make matters worse, in my early childhood, we were Southern Baptists to the core – no drinking, church on Sunday *and* Wednesday (and sometimes Sunday night just in case!), suits to church so Jesus could admire our wardrobes, etc. Dogmatic Christian groups are guilty of excessive certainty about countless uncertain things, like how long it took the world to be created, where the precise line is between those who are "saved" and "unsaved," and that hell is a real place where anyone who hasn't "accepted Jesus as his/her savior" is going. Middle-school-Southern-Baptist-Tim, who had outgrown his fear of being left by his parents, needed some new way to be petrified of abandonment and isolation. Eternal damnation seemed like just the right thing for my brain to grab ahold of.

***

It was hard enough to be certain that all of the germs were off my hands after I washed them or that my parents knew the precise time and parking place where I expected to be picked up. But at least I could see the soap suds supposedly doing their magic on my hands, and at least I could ask my parents endless questions about the timing of their return. When it came to my certainty that God loved me, however, attaining certainty became trickier.

There was no lack of certainty spewing from the authority figures in my life. Be it at home, at First Baptist of Atlanta, or at my very conservative Christian school, conversations about the afterlife went something like this:

"What about people who have never heard of Jesus? Do they go to hell?" I asked.

"Yes, Tim. That's why Christians are supposed to be spreading his message," one of the adults would reply.

"Well then why aren't all Christians missionaries to Kazakhstan?"

"That's a good question, Tim. Maybe more Christians should be."

"What about those tribes in Africa in the National Geographic magazines? What if no one has ever told them about Jesus?"

"Yes, they will go to hell if they haven't accepted Jesus, Tim...Why don't we talk about something else?!"

"But what about babies? Do they go to hell, too?"

"Well, no one knows for sure, but you're not a baby and you're not dead, so don't worry yourself too much about it. Let's talk about something else!"

You can see two things from these sorts of conversations:

1. I was a fun-filled eleven-year-old.
2. This whole eternal damnation was like a state fair for my brain – years of fun with these questions lay in store for me.

How could I possibly be sure of this salvation I wanted so desperately to attain? I had been told it was a simple matter of "accepting Jesus," which usually meant saying a prayer like this: "Dear Jesus, I am a sinner. I need your forgiveness and your grace. Thank you for dying for me to save me from my sins. I accept you as my Savior." In Christian circles, saying this prayer supposedly marks the starting point of salvation. In Southern Baptist churches, they have "altar calls" at the end of each service. People are asked to be brave enough to stand up and walk to the front of the church to publicly announce their intention of receiving salvation. The number of "converts" in a church is measured by how many people say this particular prayer.

During middle school, I must have said it over a million times.

Every day.

***

Mine was a childhood with little room for gray areas. Every question had a spiritual answer written in bold, black-and-white script (or maybe red script since that's what Jesus wrote his words in). Right was right; wrong was wrong. Right earned me praise and affection. Wrong earned me a spanking. In my Christian bubble, heaven was for the good boys while hell was for the bad boys – God's eternal spanking. But it sure seemed a lot harder to tell if God was happy with me than if my earthly authority figures were upset. How in the world could I be *certain* that I was on God's good side?

I couldn't.

How could I possibly *know* I was saved? What was the magic code to make sure I had said the right prayers, done the right things, felt the right amount of guilt for my sins? What was I supposed to feel about God if I was saved? Would a true Christian keep on sinning? After all, there's that verse that says, "Dear friends, if we deliberately continue sinning after we have received knowledge of the truth, there is no longer any sacrifice that will cover these sins" (Heb. 10:26 NLT). That's a darn scary verse for a middle schooler with OCD. Thinking I'd much rather be safe than sorry with my eternal destiny at stake, I began to say the "sinner's prayer" repeatedly.

Ten, twenty, fifty, one hundred times a day. I would tell a story wrong, think perhaps I had sinned by lying and say the prayer. I might look at a girl and feel something a little different than mere friendship, think I had lusted for her, and say the prayer again. Once, the girl sitting next to me dropped her answer sheet during a math test. Naturally distracted as the paper floated to the floor, I happened to see the answer to a question that was giving me trouble. I spent the rest of the test panicking about whether or not it would be a sin to put down the same answer she had put. "I was leaning toward that answer anyway," I thought. "But that's cheating, Tim. That's a sin, and if you sin, you'll have to say the prayer an extra million times today; then you'll have to confess to the principal because of all the guilt; then you'll probably get in big trouble at school, not to mention at home. Better leave it blank just in case." Then I said the prayer a few times just because I had even considered copying the girl's answer. Three minutes later…well, you get the picture.

***

This fear of losing my salvation created other internal compulsions, too. Knowing that 666 was the devil's number, I devised 731 as God's number. Here was my thinking: 7 seems to be universally thought of as a good or lucky number. 3 is the number of the Trinity as well as the number of days between Jesus's death and resurrection. And 1 represented that I served only 1 God. Hundreds of times an hour, the number 666 would pop into my head. I would always say internally, "Not 666, but 731; not 666, but 731." An alternative to repeating the numbers was reciting a phrase. Any time a remotely "devilish" thought came to my mind, I would repeat, "Jesus rocks; Satan sucks" over and over again to calm my fear of having worshipped the devil accidentally.

My brain activity went something like this:

- 2 sinner's prayers because I said it wrong the first time.
- Not 666! 731!!!! 731, that's right. 731. Take that, Satan.
- Another sinner's prayer because I forgot to say "Amen" after the second one.
- Jesus rocks; Satan sucks. You heard me, Satan. You suck. Jesus rocks!
- Repeat ad nauseam while awake, and if I woke up in the night, repeat then too.

***

Periodically – just often enough to keep me thinking I was actually normal – I would get a hint that maybe everyone else's brains were working just like mine. I went to camp only once in my life, the summer after 8th grade. Sometime during the month-long stay, we had a Christian singer come and entertain us for the evening. It was one of those "mountaintop experiences" one seems to always have at camp. The sort of evening when you are 100% sure that, even when you go back home, you'll break up with the unhealthy girlfriend and quit swearing forever. You'll convert your whole school to Christ with your unending zeal for the truth. You'll be like Moses coming off the mountain, glowing for all to see.

During the concert, a camp friend came over to me and we "had a moment" – the sort where you both say something vulnerable about how great God is and how much you're going to be different from here on out. My friend actually said the words that were never far from my brain: "Man, Satan sucks!"

"Wait," I thought, "did he just say what I think he said?! He's thinking it too, just like me. Everyone must be thinking it! I'm actually not any different from everyone else. They're all thinking about being eternally damned just as much as I am. It's okay. I'm NORMAL!"

Then the bubble would burst in my face the next day when I would see that same friend and try to hint at our bonding moment from the night before about how bad Satan sucks, He, of course, couldn't even remember what I was referring to. Like countless people from whom I have sought reassurance, his look would confirm that I was/am indeed insane. At that moment, I'm sure, yet again, that I'm alone, that I'm crazy, that no one else is worried about becoming accidentally possessed by the devil. No one else is convinced that, when the number 666 flashes through his brain (6,984 times an hour), that it's the devil taking over and that they only way he can be warded off is by repeating the number 731 again. No one else says the sinner's prayer every single time he thinks he might've committed a teeny tiny little sin. No one else spent the entirety of middle school petrified that eternal damnation was one unwitting sin away. At least no one who doesn't have OCD.

Chapter 4: The Joy (or Absolute Dread, in my Case) of Sex

During high school, for the only time in my memory, OCD sat in the back seat for a while. I was still unusually fearful at night, but early on my mom had given me my trusty talisman for that: "Perfect love casts out fear" was the internal (and very repetitive) radio station playing every night in my head as I sought sleep. But other than that, I was done being scared of abandonment and thought what a sissy I had been to ever have felt that way. I was done reciting the sinner's prayer (okay maybe a couple of times a week, but those were necessary, I swear!). I was done saying "731, not 666" and "Jesus rocks and Satan sucks." I was perhaps a bit more insecure than most about my friendships, somewhat obsessively seeking reassurance that my friends still liked me, but it wasn't overwhelming. If I've ever felt close to normal, this was the time. It wasn't perfect, but I felt somewhat sane. In my mind this was proof that my childhood quirks had been just small signs of immaturity – something everyone probably went through. Finally, now that I was maturing, those silly ideas were gone.

So off to college I went, ready to do the two things I had come to believe were critical to my adult life: 1. Convert the world to Christianity since everyone else, in my warped mind, was headed for hell. 2. Find a beautiful, pure, godly soul mate and start living happily ever after.

***

One of the consequences of a conservative Christian upbringing is the belief that certain sins are worse than others. The two predominant sins that, in my mind, set apart the "heathens" from the good guys were sexual sins and sins of teenage rebellion (drinking and drugs, to be exact). In youth groups, we were told time and time again both how bad drinking was and how great sex within marriage will be if only we will keep ourselves completely pure for our spouses, who will obviously do the same for us. In my social circle, we looked down on those who partied in the traditional teenage sense of the word. We saw ourselves as the good ones – the ones who chose PG movies on a Friday night rather than a raid on our parents' liquor cabinet (which, in my case, would've been empty at the time).

For me, drinking and drugs were easy to avoid. I wasn't even offered alcohol until I was in college, and by then, I had dogmatically decided that the first sip of alcohol would cause me to lose my ability to "witness" to everyone on campus. I "just said 'no,'" (thank you, Nancy Reagan), and frankly, the temptation wasn't even that strong.

But on the sexual front, things were different. Here was a very real temptation, and one I had not fared quite as well in. I was still a virgin, at least in the physical sense of the word, but saying "no" to these temptations came much less easily

41

to me. I had behaved like your average teenage boy since hitting puberty, but at this point in my life, I still defined virginity as merely a physical reality – something I no longer do. Shoot, a prostitute may well be more pure than I am. There's far more to purity than which parts of one's body have been touched and which have not.

Regarding sexual purity, my OCD had a heyday. The messages I had received about sexual purity had been branded on my broken brain, leaving an imprint of terror about ruining the best thing this life has to offer – marital sex. From my home to Bible study groups to church sermons to Christian summer camp, I had been scared into sexual purity via the notion that everything I did with someone other than my future spouse would become eternally tainted, destroying my ability to enjoy the beauty of marital sex.

I don't think my OCD was the only contributor to this belief. I've talked to many Christians who have/had the exact same ideal in mind. Heck, I think our whole society shares the idea that romantic love is the pinnacle of human existence. For secular folks, the stigma of sex outside of marriage is removed, but every magazine on the grocery store shelves sells the idea that sex, love, and romance are essentially heaven on earth.

My brain took the messages about sex and rebellion and turned them into "The Four Extra Commandments":

Rule #1: Don't have sex until you're married (okay, I know that's one of the original ones, depending on your definition of adultery).

Rule #2: Don't get divorced.

Rule #3: Don't drink until you're 21.

Rule #4: Don't turn out to be a homosexual.

I have no doubt that my obsessive brain made these messages far more dramatic and essential than was intended. Nevertheless, to this day, despite the fact that a gay man performed my wedding ceremony, despite the fact that alcohol no longer is taboo in my family, despite the fact that all of our views on divorce have softened quite a bit, and despite the fact that I have come to believe that virginity is much more of an emotional state than a physical one, I still cling inexplicably to these rules. These are cardinal sins in my mixed-up brain.

But notice that three of the rules have to do with sexuality and marriage. Somehow in my mind, I think the message my warped brain created was this: "All of your crazy fears will go away once you find the person you will marry. She will, unquestionably, have followed the same rules since they are clearly as important to God as the 10 Commandments. If you make it to marriage with these principles intact, you will be saved. All will be well."

***

So, after my blissful reprieve from OCD in high school, off to college I went with the notion that I would find my soulmate and live happily ever after. I had never thought about my life beyond college to much of an extent, though I was very sure I'd be married to a girl who aged beautifully, gave me 2.2 beautiful kids, wanted to live in a quaint home on a tree-lined street, loved the same TV shows I loved, hated the same restaurants I hated, and whose mood perfectly complemented mine no matter the situation. Together, we would set about saving the world around us. We'd be everybody's favorite friends. We'd host game nights where deep theological discussions would break out, ending with all the lost neighbors on their knees saying the sinner's prayer I knew so well. People would fight over us to go with them on vacations, and they'd stand in awe of our ability to strike the ideal balance between play and seriousness. Neighbors would use our kids as the models when yelling at their own kids: "Why can't you be more like that Johnny Blue?! He's much more _____ (fill in the adjective) than you are!" As we heard these reprimands spilling out of neighboring windows, my wife and I would smile self-satisfied smiles and pat each other on the back; or maybe we'd stop and say a brief prayer that this neighbor would come to our next game night where they'd inevitably be saved by night's end.

Many people believe in romantic love as a sort of savior; I'm certainly not alone in that regard. But as my readers may know, for someone with OCD, vacuuming a room, driving to work, washing our hands, or falling in love are all fraught with potential pitfalls. For my part, the romanticized notion of what love ought to be has been the root of the version(s) of OCD that have plagued me since my sophomore year of college, when my OCD returned with a vengeance. It has yet to go away again. I'm thirty-six.

***

It began with a fear of impotence.

Let me be quite blunt: I had no reason to fear my inability to get an erection. I had averaged 8,000-10,000 a day since puberty. Suddenly, though, this thought hit me: "What if my wedding night arrives…this night I've been told since childhood to save myself for…this night that has been my motivation for only kissing girls up to that point and nothing more (okay a little more, but not without consuming guilt that followed because I was convinced that my wife would be as pure as the driven snow and that I had now gone far past any boundary she, in her perfect purity, had ever crossed)…this night when the rest of my life begins, when things finally come into perfect alignment, when I have found someone who always understands where I am coming from, who always has patience with my moods, whose moods I find cute, not annoying…What if I get to this consummational moment, my clothes come off and…well…nothing? In despair, my new bride and I will wonder if we'll ever be able to do the thing we've been waiting for all our lives. This moment that is supposed to be the climax (pun intended) of life will be the nadir, the low point, the brink of hell itself."

I am reminded of the episode of *Seinfeld* where George gets a massage from a male masseuse and "thinks *it* moved." He spends the rest of the episode obsessing about whether or not he's gay. In my case, it wasn't the homosexuality that concerned me. It was the fear that *it* might *not move* at the right moment. How could I possibly be certain that, when the time came, the most important post-puberty member (again, pun intended…I can't resist) of my body would fail me.

This fear became a constant companion any time I didn't have a girlfriend (more on that in a minute). I remember sitting in a small group Bible study with four of five friends and telling them, as embarrassed as I've ever been, about this fear. I thought perhaps if I confessed it openly, shared it, the power of the fear would break. This was before I knew I had OCD. I still thought I had some sort of spiritual problem that needed to be solved. I must not have been praying enough, or maybe I didn't have enough faith to overcome this sort of demon. I sought and sought the spiritual answers to my fears. When they would wane years down the road, I assumed I had matured enough spiritually that I had won that battle. I never realized that the next battle was actually the same battle – one with chemicals in my brain, not demons from hell or some sort of punishment from God.

After sharing with my Bible study friends, they agreed to pray for me, and one joked that perhaps they should lay hands on the affected part of my body so I could receive healing. They didn't lay hands on "me" but they did pray for me while I sat there, utterly humiliated at having asked.

***

Having a girlfriend was the cure for this fear of impotence. But it wasn't for a good reason. The obsessions that accompanied having a girlfriend were far, far more daunting and all-consuming. In college, when I met a girl I'll call Sarah, I thought I had found "the one." She looked the part of the girl I had thought I would marry. We met at the beginning of the summer and dated for the summer. When I went away to London the next fall to study abroad, we decided to give the long distance thing a go. We survived that as well, and by the time I got back, we had been "dating" for over twice as long as I'd ever dated anyone (never mind that four of the months were completely spent apart, talking once a week on the phone). Suddenly, based on the fact that we had been "together" for six months, my brain switched gears. "Here it is," my brain whispered, "the one. This is what you've been waiting for since those darn hormones took over your life. Heck, even before that in a more innocent way. This is The Girl. Don't screw it up, Tim. Your dreams are on the threshold of coming true. Be careful. Make sure you get these next few months just right, and you'll be all set – ready to pop the question when the time is right, ready to ride off into the sunset."

In my fairy-tale reality, I had always been of the belief that it would be necessary for a serious couple to be completely honest about their past "moral failures." Couldn't a perfectly loving couple forgive anything? Plus, I was sure that I would have much more to share than the pure-as-the-driven-snow girl of my dreams, the girl who would finally rescue me from my crazy fears.

About a month after my return from overseas, we sat on Sarah's dorm-room futon and had "the talk" about our sexual history. I went in thinking, "If she could still accept me after I told her how many girls I'd kissed and that occasionally I might've gone a teensy bit further, we'll be ready to live happily ever after. We'll know it all, forgive it all, and experience the bliss of being fully known and accepted." I never thought of how I would handle her revelations; I was only worried about how she would receive mine. I had built The Ideal Woman into someone who would never possibly have anything damning to share during this "all-important" conversation. Mine was an ideal that no one could ever attain – not Sarah, not my future wife, probably not even Mother Theresa (I hear she was quite the party girl before becoming a nun!).

My whole white-picket-fence world was crushed by her revelations of having succumbed to the very same temptations I had given into. Suffice it to say that, while Sarah had less to share than most people our age, she still had things to share. I don't even know that it would've mattered if all she had ever done was to hold someone's hand on the playground near the monkey bars in third grade. My brain was ready for a new playground, and it found one in Sarah's former boyfriends.

My dream for my perfect future was destroyed. I'm not exaggerating when I say that that conversation was as painful as any I've ever experienced – that's how convinced I was that my own beliefs about sexual purity were paramount to my future happiness. It was the moment in the game of Jenga when that piece comes out that sends the whole tower to the ground, but it happens in slow motion. The tower is done for and all you can do is watch it crumble. Trouble was, this was my life, not Jenga.

Seeing how devastated I was by her mistakes, she asked if I wanted to break up. I knew enough to know that I shouldn't do that. I knew I should forgive her for having dared to make similar mistakes to my own. In my pride, I thought that maybe our story would become the reverse story of the Beauty and the Beast. I would be the magnanimous Christian man who was noble enough to forgive this woman for her failures, and our story would become legendary among the youth groups we would lead together. I would inspire the boys and girls who, like me, had to die to themselves for the sake of a partner who had failed to be 100% faithful to God as she navigated the sexually charged world of teenage-hood.

I'm well aware that my behavior was equally as bad as hers and, of course, that my judgment of Sarah was far worse than her past (relatively innocuous) behavior. But at the moment, unaware of the wayward nature of my obsessive brain, I thought I had a spiritual hill to climb. I thought God was teaching me to forgive, to lay down my life for my would-be wife (Ephesians 5:25). Not knowing that my faith had nothing to do with the obsessions, I did the best I could and tried to forge ahead with this romance that would never be as good as the one in my dreams.

Not shockingly, my brain found this new information to be a playground unlike any other. My obsessions turned against Sarah as images of her past mistakes never left my brain for even a split second. When we were together, I tried to see past the horrific images that were growing more and more monstrous by the day in my brain – images of her in pornographic scenes with nameless, faceless other guys. When we were apart, I tried to pray enough to forgive her, tried to find the right philosophy that would enable me to see her as I knew God saw her, berated myself for not being able to let go of this anger. I tried to reason with myself: "Countless others have done what she's done…and worse, Tim. Get over it."

I tried forcing my brain to think of something else. When an image came to my head, I tried replacing it with innocuous images of puppies frolicking in the park or the sun setting behind majestic mountains. But the frolicking puppies somehow became Sarah and a past boyfriend rolling around on her bed. The mountains turned into…well, you get the picture. There I was trying to take my mental walk on the beach and low and behold, Sarah and Faceless-Jerk-Who-Robbed-Me-of-My-Dream was mocking me as he did terrible things with her.

I tried the tactic of talking it through more thoroughly with Sarah. We had multiple conversations every week, trying to fix what I was feeling. I thought if I only knew more details my brain wouldn't run away imagining what might've happened in her past.

Bad idea.

I asked for details. She dutifully, ashamedly, answered my questions. Only now my brain had even more ammo to use against her, against me. I couldn't look at her without loathing and disgust. I berated myself for my lack of forgiveness, but my brain simply wouldn't (couldn't) help itself.

Eight months later, we sat on the couch in my parents' home and, after yet another conversation to fix whatever was wrong with our relationship, she asked, "Is there just something wrong that you can't put your finger on? Should we just take a break?"

Taking a break sounded good. My brain needed a break! And it didn't sound as final as a break up.

We "took a break." We tried to remain friends. I even went on vacation with her family the day after the "break," just as friends. Well, we all know that doesn't work. We were done.

My brain was relieved. Oh so relieved. Must have meant she wasn't the one for me! "Thank God for that 'growing experience,'" I thought. I was back in a peaceful place.

Until I started thinking about my future impotence – just the flip side of those haunting images of Sarah's sexual history: the fear of something ruining the white-picket-fence life I felt destined for.

Chapter 5: Till Death (or Tim's Insanity)
Do Us Part

Over the following four years, I did not date anyone seriously. I dabbled in some four or five-date romances here and there, but I never got far enough along with anyone after Sarah to bring back that version of OCD. I became convinced that it had been connected to Sarah because she had been the Wrong One. It must've been God's way of telling me to veer in a different direction.

Keep in mind that this is still years before I knew I had OCD. At this point in my life, I was treating all of this as some sort of confusing cosmic guidance. These fears and anxieties must have been God's way of telling me things; I just couldn't quite figure out what he was saying. "But," I told myself, "That's part of the journey…the mystery of knowing God. He wants me to 'seek so I will find him.' He 'disciplines those he loves,' right? So, he's just molding me into something better – probably into the guy I've dreamed of being: the perfect husband, the ideal dad, the heroic mentor to wayward young people, the friend everyone has dreamed of having. Keep seeking him, Tim. This is all part of his plan. God works in mysterious ways, and this is just his mysterious way inside of you."

So my bored brain reverted to its old companion – the fear of a flaccid future.

***

In 2002, I met Ann in a bar. She is always quick to correct that we were technically on a sidewalk outside of a bar, not in a bar. I'm not sure how that makes the story better to say that we met on a street corner, but she prefers to make a note of that. We talked (in a bar, not on the street corner) for more than an hour.

I was smitten. She was (is!) beautiful, she was classy enough to turn my obnoxious friend down when he initially hit on her, and she was the sober driver for her drunk friends. As I have always done, I instantly turned her into the saint I had been looking for. I got her number, waited all of twenty-four hours to call her and ask her out. I called a second time because I couldn't wait all evening to see if she would call back (smooth, I know). We went out the next weekend and had a nearly perfect first date. It was perfect. She was perfect. This was IT.

Given that we had been on *one* great date, my OCD decided we should go ahead and get that pesky conversation about our sexual history out of the way ASAP. My brain's habit of getting just a wee bit ahead of itself decided there was no point in putting off this all-important, happiness-determining conversation any longer.

With the deftness and subtlety of a birthing rhinoceros, I wrestled the conversation around to this topic. This poor girl I had known for a week sheepishly shared openly with me. Despite my experience with Sarah, I was still married to the notion of finding eternal happiness in the all-encompassing purity of my future mate. Like Sarah, Ann had things to share, but thanks to the mishandling of the same conversation with Sarah, I handled this one much better than the one with Sarah.

After the conversation with Ann about our past "transgressions," my spiritual viewpoint shifted as I once again tried to determine what sort of divine guidance God was offering. I came to believe that my previous experience with Sarah had paved the way for me to handle this conversation the way I should have. I was proud of myself. I went to bed that night thanking God for finally revealing why I had been through so much pain and suffering with Sarah – it was all in preparation for meeting Ann…Sarah had had to suffer from my "unforgiveness" so that Ann could be treated magnanimously. "Way to go, God," I thought. "You have prepared me to live happily ever after with Ann. You have allowed me (and Sarah) to suffer in the past so that I might be ready to be The-Guy-I've-Always-Wanted-To-Be with Ann. Now I get it. Now I'm all set for the future of my dreams!"

Uh, no.

The next day, smack dab in the middle of a lesson I was teaching, the "Sarah version" of OCD got reawakened and hit me like a Mack truck. The same images that haunted me with Sarah roared back to life with Ann at the center. Once the thoughts had plowed me over, they continued going back and forth to make sure they could do as much damage as possible before I (or the relationship) was dead.

I did a better job of hiding my obsessions from Ann while we dated than I had done from Sarah. The conversation came up a few times, and it took a small toll, but while it was wreaking havoc inside my head, I did what I had become quite good at doing over the course of twenty plus years fighting the battle – I hid it. And pretty well I might add. I had become very accomplished at hiding my real self. As a child, I learned how to craft conversations to seek reassurance about my obsessive fears, trying to mask the shame I had felt beginning when I walked into the Hardee's to find my parents on a Sunday morning. As an adult, I had hidden my embarrassing fears and obsessions behind a façade of having it all together. I dressed well, laughed at just the right moments in social situations, made great conversation with socially awkward people, made friends from all different social walks so I could put on my show for different audiences, and mastered the art of keeping a calm exterior while consuming hidden compulsions raged inside.

In short, I was an imposter. I still am.

***

During the time Ann and I were dating, my sister was getting divorced…breaking one of Tim's Four (okay three) Extra Commandments. Oddly, at least in my mind, my parents were supporting her, loving her through the pain of a broken marriage. Perhaps someone with a normal brain might have put all this information together and realized that my family was actually growing through this experience – that the dogma of conservative Christianity was showing its inevitable cracks. The real world was creeping in. When push came to shove, my parents were actually supporting, even encouraging, my sister who was in crisis. They were showing the unconditional love I was worried didn't exist.

Instead of finding relief, however, my brain doubled down, clinging to the old rules: "Don't screw up, Tim, or else. Now the pressure is even more on you to keep it all together, to show the world that you have it together. The chink in the family armor was a minor one, but it's fixed now. Keep going, and KEEP IT TOGETHER."

This fear added intense pressure to my already-exploding brain regarding whether to move forward in my relationship with Ann. I felt strongly that she was right for me, but my OCD and my sister's divorce made me even more fearful than one might ordinarily be when considering marriage. I could barely tell which end was up; trying to reason my way through the quandary did no good. To the obsessive brain, reason is a dangerous foe – one that I could spend years wrestling with, even decades, if I allowed myself to reason without ultimately forging ahead despite my obsessions.

It was time to act, and I wanted to propose to Ann.

***

My parents were more than a little skeptical when I told them I was going to propose to Ann. Rather than being a conversation filled with congratulations and joy, the conversation was filled with lots of questions and unhappy tears. Ann didn't fit the mold I had been told to pursue. My dissent from the family standards was met with resistance and the threat of rejection.

As a people pleaser, my fears grew worse. Now it was impossible to keep everyone happy. I had to choose between the girl I loved and the parents I had spent every waking moment of my life trying to please. There was no way forward that didn't involve immense danger – the danger of losing something/someone(s) who meant everything to me.

I proposed to Ann. Like anyone with OCD, I hoped that this new stage of life would bring relief to my ever-questioning brain, but just as the conversation with Sarah on her dorm-room futon had given my OCD a new avenue, singling out the woman I would marry added fresh fuel to the fire. This particular "fire" actually is common enough that it has a name: Relationship OCD (ROCD). (There's even a book about it called *Sleeping with ROCD*, by D.M. Kay - a great book actually that hits the nail on the head about the internal contents of my brain over the past ten years.)

Here's a small snapshot of the uncertainty my brain latched onto now: "How can I possibly know for sure that Ann is the perfect mate for me? Let's analyze the pros and cons:

"Pros: She is just the right mix of cute and beautiful; she is a Christian, but not one of those crusty Christian girls I have grown tired of. She's beautiful. Her faith is new, genuine, and refreshing. She is a great balance for my future-mindedness. She lives solidly in the present. She is athletic. She allows me to "be the guy," whatever that means…just the right balance of progressive and conservative in her social views.

"Cons: She doesn't fit the mold quite perfectly. She isn't one of the two or three girls about whom my parents, with a wink and a nudge, have always said, 'Hey Tim, what about so-and-so?! She'd be a great girl for you!' She doesn't know all of the Sunday School answers about why God behaves the way he does – the answers we are going to give those neighbors when they come over for game night and a theological discussion breaks out. And then there's that mole above her lip that sometimes gives me a funny tickle when we kiss. I can't stop worrying about whether I like that or not.

"But then again, I kind of like that she's not quite the It Girl my parents always pointed out. I kind of like her spiritual newness. I kind of like that she allows me to be myself, warts and all, without judgment. I kind of love her, too.

"But then again, there is that mole, and sometimes it pokes me in a funny way when we kiss. Not sure I can live with that forever. Right now it's cute – something that models get paid a lot of money to have on their faces. But what if it becomes some sort of a giant Nanny McPhee, wart-like mole with hairs growing out of it? Maybe I could hint for her to have it removed. How should I bring it up? Surely every single kiss from the Perfect-Girl-for-Me would be like the final kiss in every romantic comedy ever made with fireworks and eternal bliss and puppies frolicking and other couples admiring our perfection. Maybe I should look at it from an outsider's perspective…What do other people think of her mole? Some people call those beauty marks, but what if someone doesn't think it's attractive? I'm supposed to be married to Miss Perfect, the girl every other guy in the world wanted to marry but I "caught." Are other guys looking at me with appropriate envy? How can I tell? This mole might be the sign that God wants me to move on to someone else. Do I like the mole? Do I hate the mole? How can I possibly make the right decision about Ann when this mole is in the way?"

Lather, rinse, repeat about any and all miniscule components of our relationship.

For ten years.

God bless my infinitely patient wife. I would have divorced me a long time ago. Instead, she has chosen to stick with me, to try to realize that my OCD is not who I really am. It's very hard on both of us, but I am infinitely grateful for a true partner to walk through this insane battle with.

***

Not long before I had met Ann, God had shown up in my life, taking the shape of a sixty-year-old, Christian, gay man who told me of his own life-long battle with anxiety. Walter (not his real name) had been fighting his own inner sexual battle while surrounded by the same conservative, black-and-white Christianity I had grown up with.

Like me, Walter suffered from an affliction that was unacceptable in conservative Christian circles. The irony of the Christian bubble is that one comes into it because of his recognition that he isn't perfect. However, once inside, he must put on the front of perfection in order to remain inside. And if he's going to show the chinks in his armor, there are some struggles that are certainly off limits for the truly saved: homosexuality and mental illness fell squarely within this category. While they are growing to be more acceptable forms of weakness, the more conservative realms of Christianity are still fighting hard against the notion that one can be saved and have certain unmentionable temptations or flaws.

Like me, Walter had tried to use his faith to escape his struggle. He had "confessed" to some close friends and asked for prayer. He had been anointed with oil and prayed over in hopes of being healed. He had fasted and prayed on his own. And all to no avail. He still preferred men over women.

And like me, Walter still clung to the essence of his faith. Despite the wounds inflicted by the church, Walter still wanted to follow God. He still believed that heterosexuality was God's original design, so he remained celibate.

I have infinite respect for Walter both for his celibacy and for his honesty. I was twenty-five years old when we met, and Walter was the first Christian I had ever known who demonstrated that it was okay to be broken. Here was a man struggling with something "worse" (in the eyes of conservative Christianity) than my affliction but who was willing to open up and be honest about it. For me, this was radical and revolutionary. But where were the others like him? Where was the church where I could find people like Walter? People who battled unmentionable struggles like drug and alcohol addiction, mental illness, divorce, or homosexuality. To me, church had always been a place where I had to put on my costume of perfection in order to attend. I was more likely to find empathy for my struggles in a bar than in a church. For the most part, that's still the case.

***

In one of our early conversations, Walter changed my life in a different way, too. He told me about his diagnosis of Generalized Anxiety Disorder. He told me about medication. I had absolutely no idea that such a diagnosis existed, nor that medication existed. From what I knew, psychiatrists and medications were for people who were certifiably crazy, people who meowed when they saw chickens or who ate carpet cushions, people who didn't have Jesus in their lives to fix all that was wrong with them.

Walter insisted that I go see a psychiatrist and he made me promise that I would give medication a try for at least eighteen months before giving up on it. I obeyed, desperate. And while my medication journey has been difficult, even landing me in the psychiatric hospital at one point, it has unquestionably saved my marriage and even my life.

More on the medication journey later, but what happened over the coming months was one of those ordinary mundane miracles that I've come to believe in far more than the walking-on-water sort I used to think I could expect. After I fired my first psychiatrist for being too expensive, I found a psychiatrist who prescribed Effexor. Nothing magical happened, but in the coming months and years, I actually began to think my OCD had gone away. At this point, despite having finally been diagnosed with OCD, I was still dubious about it being a real thing, and I was equally dubious about the possibility of medication helping the problem. I was just obeying my friend, Walter.

A couple of peaceful years later, I thought I had finally won the battle with those darn demons. I was happily married. My parents seemed to have made peace with (even to like) my choice of a partner, and all was well. I genuinely believed that the medication was irrelevant – I just thought I had finally found my white-picket-fence. I even told my psychiatrist I wanted to go off the meds. He looked at me knowingly and said, "I'm pretty sure it's the medication that's helping you. I wouldn't recommend it. You will probably need to stay on Effexor forever, Tim."

"No, no," I said, "I need to give it a try. I don't want to be on medicine forever. I'm in a better place now than when I came to you. I'll be fine without it."

"Okay, it's up to you," he said, undoubtedly having had this conversation many, many times before.

I went off the meds…not a good move.

Gradually, the obsessions took over once again. Things I had been able to let go of while on Effexor became insurmountable obstacles between me and peace. Ann grew frustrated as I insisted on rehashing ideas over and over to tweak them or to gain reassurance about various and sundry inane issues. The monster that had controlled my first twenty-five years was rearing its head once again.

The what ifs crawled back inside my brain: What if I'm in the wrong relationship? What if I can't ever get a job I like? What if I get a job I think I will like but it's in Oregon and I move out there and ruin my life, and Ann's? What if Ann decides she's had enough of me, like I nearly have? What if? What if? What if? What if? What if? What if? What if? What if? What if? What if? What if? What if? What if? What if? What if? What if? What if? What if? What

65

if? What if? What if? What if? What if? What if? What if? What if? What if? What if? What if? What if? What if? What if?

A few months later, I was back in my psychiatrist's office, sheepishly asking to go back on Effexor. He was nice enough not to say, "I told you so."

Chapter 6: Trouble in Medication Paradise

It took ten years from the time Walter told me I had to give medication a try to the moment when I finally, truly believed that I really had a medical problem that could be helped by medication. While Effexor was helping to calm my anxieties and obsessions, it was never a panacea. For me, the primary side effect of Effexor was plain old physical agitation – jitteriness, the inability to sit still, inability to concentrate, etc. Essentially, Effexor gave me ADHD while curing my OCD.

I told the psychiatrist that I couldn't sit still and couldn't concentrate as I read students' papers. Often, I would have to reread a paragraph three or four times before I felt like I had actually read it. At night, I would constantly pick at myself, trying to quell my nervous energy. He said we should test me for ADHD. So, he pulled out a piece of paper, asked me to rate certain feelings on a scale of 1-5 for ten quick questions, added up the numbers at the end, and told me I definitely had ADHD. Something inside me balked at this, just as I was still balking at my OCD diagnosis. Shouldn't there be more to an ADHD diagnosis than a two-minute questionnaire? Surely I didn't have ADHD...the kids in my elementary school who took Ritalin were those "certifiably nutty" people I was sure I wasn't like. In my family, they went into the "not so good" group…you know, people with Problems.

Nevertheless, I wanted to get rid of this constant agitation, so I went along for the ride. For this newfound ADHD, he prescribed Vyvanse, the latest version of Adderal. When I took the prescription to my pharmacist, she seemed concerned that he had prescribed 50 mg when the highest possible dose is 70 mg. "Have you ever taken this before?" she asked.

"No, why?"

"It's just an awfully high dose if you don't yet know how it will affect you. You might want to call and ask your psychiatrist if he wants you to work your way up to this dosage or if he mis-wrote the prescription."

I knew this pharmacist to be a little too willing to share her unsolicited opinions, so I blew her off, walked away with my new medication, convinced that it wouldn't do anything for me anyway. I was quite sure I didn't have ADHD since I had never had one teacher or supervisor comment on my lack of focus. Nevertheless, being a good patient, I went home and took the pill the next morning.

***

For those who don't know, ADHD medication is essentially speed…the very same drug that is sold on the streets, the same drug that, on college campuses, can be sold on the "black market" to kids who need to study all night or who just want to feel an extra high for that night's party. Let me be frank: It is AWESOME!

Within an hour of taking my first dose, I was convinced that I had stumbled upon the solution to ALL my problems. I felt calm…calmer than ever! I could focus. I was upbeat and friendly. I could finally sit still. I instantly quit picking at my fingers, and for the first time in my recollection, the constant bleeding around my fingernails stopped.

This was IT! Hallelujah! Problem solved! Unbeknownst to me, I thought, ADHD had been what was plaguing me for my whole life. I started to re-theorize my entire life history based on this new miracle drug. Perhaps OCD was just a manifestation of my ADHD. Maybe my innate inability to focus had had the effect of making my hyper-focused…a.k.a obsessive. I needed a way to explain the miracle that was Vyvanse. I felt well beyond good. I felt insanely good. I felt nearly perfect.

Once again, I talked my psychiatrist into letting me go off of Effexor and just use Vyvanse. He acquiesced, and I went home certain that all would finally be well in my brain. For good this time! I had my miracle cure, the solution to all my problems.

After a few weeks, the bloom was off the rose. The positive effects of Vyvanse were beginning to be overshadowed by badly disrupted sleep patterns and the loss of the "high" sensation I had felt when I first took it. I was sound asleep on the couch every night ("crashing" to be exact) at 8. I would stumble up to bed for the night. Then sometime around 4 a.m., I was wide awake – the kind of wide awake that even makes closing your eyes feel like hard work. I was wired!

I began to feel controlled by the drug and very out of control of my own life. I wasn't getting that miraculous jolt about an hour after taking it that I had at first. I wanted more Vyvanse. The psychiatrist pushed me up to 60 mg and told me he thought this would do the trick. It only made matters worse. Tension grew in my marriage as I was useless in the evening to help with childcare. Frustration grew inside me as I no longer had any say about when I slept and when I woke up. The weird effects of the medicine were deciding that for me.

Eventually, I quit taking it and decided to go back to square one and find a new psychiatrist – get a second (okay, third) opinion about what was really wrong with me. All I knew at this point was that I wanted to feel as good as I had those first few weeks on Vyvanse. I wanted to feel complete calm and peace and rest and focus…that bliss. Effexor had never done anything remotely like that for me.

Half of me was still convinced I just had a spiritual problem, just needed to get to know God a little better so I could truly "rest in him," as I was supposed to be doing. The other part of me desperately wanted a psychiatrist to figure out precisely why I was so anxious, to diagnose my brain in the same way they can diagnose a broken wrist or a particular kind of cancer. I wanted a psychiatrist to take control of the situation, demand that I take a certain course of action, and prove to be right in the end by fixing me. No such luck.

***

My new psychiatrist was equally as un-thorough as the previous one. He blithely listened to my story during the obligatory first hour-long meeting. He even told me, "You don't have 'OCD proper.'" He just thought I was a bit over-anxious. Always eager to seem put-together, I bought into his theory and agreed that I probably just needed something to calm my nerves a bit. To this day, I have difficulty with psychiatrists because I am so trained to put on a good show, so good at glossing over the maddening free-for-all that has plagued my brain for my entire life. Even when I do get up the guts to tell them how bad it is, half the time I don't think they believe me.

Just yesterday, a co-worker who knows of my OCD, was telling me a story about a service project at a mental health facility wherein he encountered a man who couldn't even look at others because he was so caught up in his compulsions – doing something with his hands in this case; I didn't get the details. I told him I knew how that man felt, and he looked at me as if I had said I knew how Adolf Hitler felt about the Jews. I've seen that look many times, even from doctors. They simply can't believe that, because I am polished on the exterior, I am no different from that man in the rehab facility playing with his hands. I'm never without my obsessions. I'm never without my compulsions, but they are *all* hidden from view. I am *never* paying complete attention to anything because of the incessantly screaming demons inside my head.

Anyway, this new psychiatrist believed my theory that ADHD had been the real problem all along, and he prescribed Ritalin for the day-time and Ambien for the night-time. I was on a roller coaster of highs and lows at this point. I was off kilter. I took Ritalin four or five times a day, trying to keep that blissful feeling of calm I wanted so desperately. At night, I took Ambien to kill the effect of Ritalin. Without the Ambien I was incapable of sleep. One night I didn't take it because I needed to get up early the next morning. Three hours later, I was still staring at the ceiling. Finally, I took the Ambien and went to sleep. When I awoke a few hours later, I took the Ritalin to get me going. Welcome to drug addiction, Tim.

I did drop about ten pounds in one month while on it. I was excited that a medicine that did my brain some good was also doing my waistline some good. I was ready to do an infomercial for a new weight-loss drug called Ritalin, but apparently rapid weight loss is a bad thing. At my next meeting, psychiatrist #3 told me I needed to get off of Ritalin immediately. Darn.

We tried Remeron, a plain old anti-anxiety drug. This felt like being on six times the max dose of Ambien mixed with a 5th of Scotch during the day. I was so far out of it that I couldn't do my job, couldn't even remember what question a student had just asked. I wanted an instant cure, and this was no instant cure. So, I quit that one on my own.

At my next meeting, psychiatrist #3 got really angry with me: "Everything's going to have some side-effects!" he nearly screamed. Offended, I sarcastically apologized for being such a pain. He backed down, told me it must be frustrating to feel so consumed by anxiety and asked me what I wanted to try next.

I don't even remember what I tried next, if anything, but that was my last meeting with him, partly because he had moved across town, and partly because of his outburst. Who needs a doctor who sees his patients as frustrating nuisances? I had spent my whole life feeling like I was a nuisance because of my mental health issues. No thanks. I'll try yet another psychiatrist. This would make number four.

***

Psychiatrist #4 listened much better than psychiatrists #3. His diagnosis: OCD, ADHD, and possibly a little bit of depression. He even said, "I don't know how 'psychiatrist #3' couldn't have thought you have OCD. That's rather obvious." I remained baffled as to whom I should believe, and as to whether any of these doctors were anything more than witch doctors prescribing herbal remedies to cure spear wounds in the jungle. But I was determined to stick with this one. I had fired my last two doctors. I was reeling internally, in desperate need of a mental anchor. I promised myself I'd stay the course this time, give the doctor a chance to figure things out.

Psychiatrist #4 started me on Luvox – 100mg, the first line of defense against OCD in most cases. He also added in a smaller dosage of Vyvanse – 20 mg. I was excited to try this course of action. It seemed like we were heading back down the road that had initially felt like salvation – an anti-depressant and an ADHD medication. This was finally going to be IT. Psychiatrist #4 was The Psychiatrist for me.

If you'd like to hear the rest of this part of the story, you should reread chapter 1. Luvox nearly killed me, and in retrospect, I think the Vyvanse merely kicked it up a notch. Doctors, in my experience, will admit that anti-depressants do have the "black box warning," that frightening little statement on the packaging that warns against worsening of depression and even suicidality in some patients, but in my experience, most of them simply don't believe that is a legitimate warning. Most of them will tell you that people my age won't have those side effects or that they think it's not a legitimate possibility – just something the drug companies need to put on there to cover their asses.

In the midst of the despair that landed me in the hospital, I went to see my primary care doctor, hoping he might know of a way to keep me from killing myself. His response caused me to lose most of my faith in doctors: "My theory," he said, "is that anti-depressants make people feel just enough better to go out and act on their suicidal impulses."

Take a moment and let the brilliance of that statement sink in…

Any doctor who is foolish enough to let those words come out of his mouth should immediately have all of his degrees stripped…So, what you're telling me, doc, is that people who feel like the world is black and hopeless start taking a drug that lets in a little bit of light, and their first thought is, "Phew, you know, I'm feeling better now – just enough better to finally go pick up those shotgun shells I've been needing in order to blow my brains out. Yesterday, I didn't quite feel good enough to get to Wal-Mart, but today is a better day, a perfect day for a nice suicide." Yeah, that makes sense, Doc.

So psychiatrist #4 (with a little help from my ignorant primary care physician) was the one who landed me in the psychiatric hospital. In retrospect, I think he was actually a decent psychiatrist; I am just a tough patient. I react very sensitively to anti-depressants. Every single one of them has made me feel either depression or anger, at least at first. It wasn't until much later that I learned to be my own advocate, to trust both the doctor's wisdom and my own experience. I will also say this about shrink #4: After I got out of the hospital, I wrote a scathing letter to both him and the primary care doctor who proposed the theory about people "feeling just enough better to go act on their suicidal impulses." Shrink #4 wrote me back in the most professional and compassionate of terms. He defended himself, but not without being kind and humane about the whole situation, telling me he certainly understood my desire to see someone new. The primary care doctor, on the other hand, called me to angrily defend himself via a meandering voicemail. He subsequently sent me a letter saying I could no longer be a patient at his practice. I got fired as a patient! In retrospect, I actually find that quite amusing. At the time, I did not.

***

The doctor I saw in the hospital became psychiatrist #5 once I was out of the hospital. He seemed to think I was just really, really high strung and that I mainly needed to play more tennis or something like that so I could get out my excess energy. He even told me I didn't have OCD: "People who have OCD don't leave their homes," he said. An awfully narrow view for a psychiatrist, but then again, he does work in a psychiatric hospital, so I'm sure that the people he sees who have OCD are extreme cases. Then again, I'm not so sure I'm not on the extreme end, too. I've just developed extreme coping mechanisms so I can leave my house.

Psychiatrist #5 put me on to a therapist who worked in his office, and I decided to try the Freudian route instead of the prescription route. I began seeing a therapist I'll call Dave once a week. By now, I was completely off of medication and convinced that I would never touch another anti-depressant. I was going to get to the bottom of all of this with Dave, and then I could finally get to "living happily ever after."

At this point in time, I was 33 years old, and I had managed to hide my OCD from virtually everyone in my life. My family, growing up, knew I was anxious and had some weird habits, but we never really talked directly about it. My close friends knew I had strange thoughts – like fearing impotence – but again, they thought I was just a little bit neurotic. Even Walter, the man who convinced me to see a psychiatrist, just thought I had the same thing he had – chronic anxiety. That was how I had characterized what I felt all my life. After all, OCD does come with a lot of anxiety. But I hadn't yet come out of the closet. I hadn't yet been willing to just own it. I tiptoed around it, talking about my anxiety, referring ashamedly to my visits to the psychiatrist's office, feeling constantly fearful that people just thought I was making a mountain out of a molehill, unwilling (or unable) to admit to people that I was actually crumbling inside, that I couldn't hold on much longer, that a lifetime of constant obsessions mixed with almost-entirely internal compulsions had worn me down to a nub. I was empty, but I was still clinging to my dignity, still sure that people saw me as having it all together, still sure that this was a good thing – that God couldn't "use me" for his purposes unless I maintained this façade. So, I set about fixing the problem so I could get on with my life and the business of saving the world, since I was fairly sure that was my job.

***

Dave was great...for a while. He was completely a-spiritual, and I enjoyed the freedom I felt with him. He had a lot of good things to say, and I deeply appreciated the fact that, for once, someone didn't spiritualize my struggles. He came at it from a very humanistic perspective: "You need to change your thinking habits, Tim," he said over and over. He gave me mantras to recite in the mirror, and I actually did feel a little bit of improvement for a time...I think it was called hope.

But the same old, same old reared its ugly head, and I became incapable of hiding my obsessions from my wife anymore. Trouble is, they were all about her, and as you might imagine, nitpicking every single one of your wife's "flaws," convinced that the outfit that didn't quite "work" or the strand of gray hair that was showing or the bodily changes that came with/after pregnancy meant I had married the wrong girl, doesn't do good things for a marriage. Our white picket fence was broken, and to my mind, it must've been her fault. Maybe if I could just get her to correct these little things that were wrong, the dream life could still be mine. I abandoned my strategy of keeping my obsessions to myself.

This did not go well.

I began to mention things to Ann that I had been keeping to myself for many years. I asked her to change certain outfits, even to get rid of certain clothes because every glimpse of her in them sent my brain into overdrive, forced me into my mental gymnastics for hours, days, or even weeks.

Eventually the day would come when she would "look the part" of the perfect person I was supposed to marry, and my brain would calm down again…until she changed clothes, that is.

We sought counseling. The Christian counselor told me I wasn't being a very good "Ephesians 5:25 sort of husband," loving my wife the way Christ loved the church. I looked at her so angrily that she asked what I was thinking. "No one gets it," I said. "I'm trying SO DAMN HARD to be just that sort of a husband to my wife. That's all I want to be, all I've ever wanted to be. I'm doing everything in my power to love my wife, but my brain is getting in the way!" To the counselor's credit, she apologized.

But still, like anyone who is free of OCD, she didn't get it…couldn't get it. She just thought I needed to try harder, pray a bit more, read the Bible again, get right with God, etc. Like I had believed for most of my life, she thought I had a spiritual problem, not a chemical problem. By this time, I was finally ready to stand up for myself, to say, "You're missing the boat! I already know what a Godly husband is supposed to think and do. I just can't get my brain to stop its roaring mayhem!"

***

While Ann and I sought couples counseling, I kept working individually with Dave. Dave told me over and over that all of these concerns about Ann really boiled down to my own inability to stand on my own two feet. He seemed to think that I had failed to rebel against my upbringing in a healthy way (he was actually right about that) and that I still needed to give my past the proverbial finger and blaze my own trail. We spent a lot of time talking about my parents' initial disapproval of Ann and about my need to actively rebel against them for once. He gave me pep talk after pep talk about "going my own way," but in the end, no amount of pep talks could cure a mental illness. I couldn't stop thinking the same old thoughts. Literally. In the middle of the night, I was analyzing my marriage. All day at work, I was analyzing my marriage. The first glimpse of Ann each morning or each day after work sent my brain reeling, evaluating, analyzing, deciphering. Was she the right one or not? I'm sure I can figure it out if I just work on the problem long enough. I like her outfit today; hair looks good; figure looks nice; people are reacting to her in a way that makes me think they like her...okay, problem solved. She's a good choice for me.

Then she would change clothes mid-day. Oh crap, I don't like that outfit. People must be wondering why I married her. Let's think this through some more to see if I might've made a mistake. Let's think this through some more to see if I might've made a mistake. Let's think this through some more to see if I might've made a mistake. Let's think this through some more to see if I might've made a mistake. Let's think this through some more to see if I might've made a mistake. Let's think this through some more to see if I might've made a mistake. Let's think this through some more to see if I might've made a mistake. Let's think this through some more to see if I might've made a mistake. Let's think this through some more to see if I might've made a mistake. Let's think this through some more to see if I might've made a mistake. Let's think this through some more to see if I might've made a mistake. Let's think this through some more to see if I might've made a mistake. Let's think this through some more to see if I might've made a mistake. Let's think this through some more to see if I might've made a mistake. Let's think this through some more to see if I might've made a mistake. Let's think this through some more to see if I might've made a mistake. Let's think this through some more to see if I might've made a mistake. Let's think this through some more to see if I might've made a mistake. Let's think this through some more to see if I might've made a mistake. Let's think this through some more to see if I might've made a mistake. Let's think this through some more to see if I might've made a mistake. Let's think this through some more to see if I might've made a mistake. Let's think this through some more to see if I might've made a mistake. Let's think this through some more to see if I might've made a mistake. Let's think this through some more to see if I might've made a mistake. Let's think this through some more to see if I might've made a mistake. Let's think this through some more to see if I might've made a mistake.

***

Dave was very helpful to me for a time – as helpful as a counselor could possibly be who wasn't treating the root issue – the chemical imbalance inside of me. But when Dave suggested that perhaps I didn't really love Ann after all, perhaps I should consider a separation, I knew our time had been used up. Now we were heading down the wrong road. But I also knew by then that my marriage was in real trouble because of my OCD. I had hurt Ann – a lot. She began to feel ashamed of herself around me. She feared getting undressed, knowing I was "surreptitiously" scrutinizing her to see if she fit the dream-girl model in my head, like I had done last night and the night before, and every chance I got, seeking FINAL PROOF that all would be well. When I arrived home from work and she was wearing sweats, she knew that the look of disapproval meant. The dream girl was always dressed up, happy to meet her man after a long, hard day of work, always smiling, always put-together. The dream girl didn't have "sweatpants days."

In what turned out to be our final meeting, even Dave told me I needed to pursue medication. He pegged me correctly, saying that I would never be able to make a reasonable decision about whether to end my marriage with my brain in its current state. He didn't call it OCD per se, but he knew that I was riddled with so much anxiety that no matter which decision I made, I would second guess it ad nauseam…you got that right, Dave! But not just second guess it. Third and fourth and fifth… and eight billionth guess it too.

***

Back to medication.

Again.

But the high I had received from Vyvanse had set me back immensely. Even to this day, I want that high again. I understand hard core drug addiction because of that experience. My first few weeks on Vyvanse were the best I've ever felt; it's hard to give up the idea of ever feeling that good again. I understand why there's a black market for Adderal! Wish I had saved some. Oh well.

In my desperation for something to help me, I started calling all the psychiatrists within a 20 mile radius. I found psychiatrist #6 and chose him merely because he had an opening that same day. Note to self: Psychiatrists who have same-day openings probably aren't very good since most of them have months-long waiting lists.

Suffice it to say that I'm not entirely sure psychiatrist #6 was playing with a full deck. Ever the people pleaser, I tried to make chit chat when I walked into his office. In plain view, he had his computer screen pulled up to some sort of website where planes seemed to be for sale. I made the mistake of asking him about this, and he rambled for five whole minutes about what sort of plane he wanted to buy. He never made eye contact, staring well above my head for the entire monologue, and he spoke in a spooky, monotone voice – almost robotically. When I would say something about my mental health, he would stare off into space for minutes, literally. I was the one who kept the conversation going, not him. I asked about taking Lexapro, which my sister and a friend had had good results with. He started to explain why Effexor would be better, but his explanation stalled after a sentence or two, and he stared blankly into space, never finishing his thought. He wrote the prescription and then sat there for minutes, staring blankly again. I had to finally ask him if there was anything else. This brought him back from wherever he was, and he handed me the prescription.

Time to look for psychiatrist #7.

***

Psychiatrist #7 gets a name because she has been my chemical savior. Dr. Zhang, at first, seemed like she would be yet another doctor to cross off the list of people who might be able to help. Mildly dubious about sharing my deepest secrets with a female doctor, it turned out that Dr. Zhang also spoke with a thick Chinese accent, making it somewhat of a challenge to follow everything she said. "Oh well," I thought, "might as well give her a chance. At least she seems coherent, unlike psychiatrist #6."

Our first meeting lasted an hour, and man did she grill me! When I finished with my spiel about being hospitalized, etc., she started to hone in on something no one had ever pointed out.

"You finished a Ph.D. in four years while working full time for three of those years and having a child, too?" she asked.

I had no idea where this was headed. "Yes," I responded. I'm very motivated when I set my mind to something.

"How did you do that? Physically, I mean," she asked.

"I got up early, multi-tasked like crazy, used every spare second, and just made it happen."

"Did you feel like you were on some sort of a high while all this was going on? Like you had extra energy or anything like that?"

Now I started to see. She was trying to determine if I had bi-polar tendencies. I did NOT want yet another diagnosis! I resisted her mightily, even confronting her train of thought.

"I can see where you're going with this," I said, "but I really don't think I'm bi-polar. I've never gone on a crazy spending spree or had rampant sex with strangers or stayed in bed for weeks like people who have bi-polar. I think you're barking up the wrong tree."

"Tim, you definitely have OCD. No one would miss that." (Uh, actually, a number of psychiatrists have missed that!). "But what I'm getting at is that there are two types of bi-polar. The kind you're describing is only one version. Bi-polar II is more what I'm thinking about. It can look like extreme productivity in some people. But these are the people who are most likely to kill themselves because no one looks at them as being mentally ill. They just have ups and downs that look like more extreme versions of everyone else's."

Then she said something that showed me that this was no ordinary know-it-all psychiatrist.

"It doesn't really matter whether you're bi-polar or not, Tim. I am here to treat your symptoms, not a diagnosis. What really matters is that we find a drug or a combination of drugs that can help your unique, beautiful brain. You're different. You're not an easy case, but we have a lot of evidence that there's more going on than simple OCD or simple depression. We need to try some new things if we're going to get to the bottom of this."

My friend, Mike, who has spent the bulk of his career in a call center working for the mental health line of a major insurance company, is deeply, deeply cynical about the field of mental health. He's seen it all, and he says it ain't pretty! A lot of psychiatrists behave just like doctors 1-6: They want to put each patient into a box, give them the latest pill for said diagnosis, and send them on their way. When I told him what Dr. Zhang said about treating symptoms, not diagnoses, he was stunned. "I've never heard anyone say that, but that's a really good way to look at it, Tim. You may have really found a great psychiatrist!"

I have.

I don't know if I could've appreciated Dr. Zhang, psychiatrist #7, unless I had been through all the ups and downs of psychiatrists 1-6, but I am deeply grateful for her. She has saved my marriage and possibly my life.

Even today, two years into our working together, my meetings with Dr. Zhang last thirty minutes, not five to ten minutes like with most other psychiatrists. Dr. Zhang asks questions, listens carefully, talks to me about stressors that I need to get rid of, counsels me, demonstrates care and compassion, loves me…and then writes me a prescription.

If this book accomplishes anything in the psychiatric world, I would hope it would be this: Psychiatrists, you need to take lessons from Dr. Zhang. You need to LISTEN to your clients. You need appointments that last more than fifteen minutes that are for the sole purpose of writing a prescription. You need to ask questions and dig beneath the surface of what your clients are saying. You need to remember the reason you went into medicine in the first place – to help people. You have an amazing opportunity. Quit being the slave of drug companies and money. Slow down.

I'll say it again: Listen.

***

None of this is to say that Dr. Zhang fixed all of my problems immediately. The medication journey has still been very rocky for me. When I first saw her, I was on a small dose of Effexor, but in our first meeting she noticed some strong bi-polar II tendencies as well. I was very dubious because in my experience, people with bi-polar go from being suicidal to buying Lamborghinis as their moods go back and forth. But she said that, for bi-polar II, one of the symptoms can look a lot like intense productivity during periods of "mania." On that front, I was guilty as charged. I have always gone through periods of intense productivity followed by periods where I don't feel like doing anything. On top of that, when I told Ann about Dr. Zhang's hunch, her reply was telling: "I've never really thought about it before, Tim, but you do have very intense mood swings. One day you're playing with the kids and happy as can be; the next, I don't even know what to do with you because you seem so despondent. Dr. Zhang might be onto something."

Because of her bi-polar hunch and my inability to sleep while on SNRI's (Serotonin-Norepinephrine Reuptake Inhibitors, as opposed to SSRI's: Selective Serotonin Reuptake Inhibitors), Dr. Zhang prescribed Seroquel – the best sleeping pill ever invented, but also an "anti-psychotic." That very terminology is terrifying to me. Psychotic?! I'm not psychotic. Psychotic people go on killing sprees. We need to change the vocabulary surrounding mental health.

Anyway, I was doing really well on these two drugs, feeling sane and somewhat happy again. Able to realize that Ann is beautiful, that she is the perfect spouse for me, and that the minutia I incessantly critiqued in my head were just that: minutia. The compulsions and mood swings weren't gone per se, but I could manage them. They took the same shape I imagine they take in many people's lives – frustrations of being a human, but frustrations that could be tamed and talked to, not ones that crept inside my body and possessed every waking moment, every sleeping moment, every cell of my being.

Turns out, though, that Seroquel has some nasty potential side-effects, and because the anti-psychotic seemed to be helping, Dr. Zhang wanted me to try switching to a tamer mood stabilizer (a nicer name for an anti-psychotic), Lamictal. Bad idea.

Lamictal made me feel angry. I mean ANGRY. Like I wanted to punch everyone I came across. I found myself actually wanting to follow the guy who cut me off in traffic to confront him when he stopped at the next light. I had to talk myself out of reprimanding people in public for talking too loud or for wearing too much perfume. I felt aggressive all the time. Not a good trait for a man with two small children who gave him many reasons to feel frustrated, angry, or aggressive.

Then we tried Abilify. I gained ten pounds in a month. It has taken over a year to get (5 of) them off. I didn't need something else to obsess about. When I went off Abilify, the depression I had felt on Luvox came creeping back in.

***

OhshitfuckgoddammitIcantdothismuchlonger!

***

I was still on a very small dose of Effexor, and I told Dr.
Zhang I was convinced it was the Effexor making me feel
depressed. My experience with Luvox still loomed (looms!)
large. I was scarred…and scared. I begged her to let me
come off of it. She did the right thing: She made me beg; she
made me explain my thinking; she challenged me, telling me
she thought I was experiencing some real depression, not a
reaction to the meds. Reluctantly, she let me try getting off
of Effexor, but Dr. Zhang was vigilant in questioning me and
in reminding me that I might be feeling some genuine
depression, not just a side-effect of the medication. She was
right, but it took me a year of trying other anti-depressants
(Zoloft, back to Effexor, Seroquel by itself, back to
Effexor…).

At one point during the year-long back-and-forth with anti-
depressants, I was pouring out the Effexor capsules and
counting pellets (there are probably 100 or so inside of a 75
mg capsule) in an effort to gain control of the titration
process. When I would take a few extra pellets in an effort to
calm my OCD, I seemed to feel my depression growing.
When I would take fewer pellets, I felt a burst of hope that
convinced me it really was the Effeoxor causing the
depression. The only other time I had felt this sort of
chemical, uncontrollable depression (as opposed to what I
call existential depression – the depression felt by all of us as
we question what life really means and why small children
have to die…) was on Luvox. So it had to be the meds,

right? Somewhere along the way, my body must've decided it hated anti-depressants and would rebel against any and all of them. Dr. Zhang was trying to get me to push higher on anti-depressants, but I was too scared to do so.

After the fiftieth attempt to get back on Effexor, I weaned myself off once again, convinced that the looming despair I felt was because of the extra three pellets I had ingested that morning. I needed to know where ground zero was once again. I had lost the sense of which end was up.

***

Once it was all out of my system, and I had nothing to blame but my brain, I realized that Dr. Zhang was, as usual, right. It wasn't the medication causing my depression. It was plain old me – off of any and all medication, no more medication-based excuses for why I wanted to jump off of a bridge. I was just plain depressed. This sort of depression feels like a physical weight, like a blanket of cosmic darkness you can't untangle yourself from. It made me feel similar things to what I felt on Luvox: distant from the world around me, unconcerned with any of the things that used to concern me on others' behalf. I felt tingly all over my body – not the pleasant tingly like when you have goose bumps, but a kind of tingly that makes you feel like demons are tickling you all over, threatening to throw you off a cliff like they did the herd of pigs when Jesus cured the demoniac. I was lost in my own world of torture and mental anguish. I just wanted it to end. No matter how.

***

Maybe Luvox just unlocked something in my brain that had been there all along; maybe Luvox added something new to the chemical malfunctions in my brain; maybe years of fighting the battle with my brain had created a new issue...who knows? But now I knew: Depression had come home to roost in my brain, complementing OCD, anxiety, and perhaps a little bi-polar II.

Depression is hell. Once I realized that I couldn't blame anti-depressants for every ounce of depression I had ever felt, I began to look at it differently. Before, I had been an innocent bystander who couldn't really relate to feelings of cosmic doom. Now it was a part of me, not just a side-effect of a medication. It lived off of my brain cells. It found a livable home inside of my spirit.

As I realized the gravity of what I was dealing with: OCD, bi-polar, depression, and anxiety, I felt defeated, both by the illnesses themselves, as they seemed to be winning the battle for my soul, and by the fear that nothing could fix all that was wrong inside my head. I was no cut-and-dried case; perhaps that was another lesson from the seven psychiatrists I had now seen. No one could quickly put a label on Tim Blue and fix him with just one ordinary drug. I became worried that even Dr. Zhang with all her patience and kindness couldn't fix what was ailing me.

Depending on how you're counting, this was either thirty-five or ten years into a journey of misery for me. I'd been battling my whole life to feel sane, but as for trying to medicate the problem, I was a mere ten years in on that one. Either way you sliced it, I felt really overwhelmed.

I was ready for a permanent solution, even one that involved me being buried. But when I thought of ending it all, one of my most primordial spiritual fears came creeping back in: If I killed myself, I might actually go to hell. Though I'm not Catholic (they believe suicide is an unforgivable sin), I had plenty of fear about who God was/is from my upbringing that I didn't want to take the chance. The same people who had sold me on God's love for me had convinced me that, if I hadn't been truly saved, I'd spend eternity in a burning pit of unending anguish. So now I was truly, completely, unavoidably screwed: literally damned if I did (kill myself) and damned if I didn't (depressed to the point that life was joyless and hopeless and meaningless and empty and burdensome and brutally cruel).

The revelation that depression was indeed a part of my chemical make-up, at least at this point in my life, brought me to a place of surrender in the journey towards medication-dependency. This was the final straw – the proof that I couldn't survive my mental battles on my own. I could no longer blame medication for being a cure that was worse than my original disease, OCD. I waved the white flag and told Dr. Zhang I was ready to be a better patient, not one who wanted to try something new every month.

***

I went back to Effexor and Seroquel, and I am still there today. I have decided that I am willing to trade some good years for the potential side effects of Seroquel. I'll cross that bridge when I get to it. For now, I need to avoid killing myself as I raise two small children and try to undo some of the hefty damage I have done to my marriage. I need to keep my job, too.

The process of getting back on full dosages of these medications was a battle that required a lot of faith. The reality is that the first few days of a new dosage of any medication are very rough for me, nearly convincing me each time to jump ship and go a different route. But when I realized that the depression or anger I was attributing to the medication was, at least in part, coming out of my own body, too, I was willing to forge ahead.

This helpful combination of drugs it is certainly not a panacea. Effexor makes me jittery. Many times a day I feel completely out of breath, like I've been punched in the stomach. I pick at myself to calm my nerves, but they are largely uncalmable, and this is a direct effect of Effexor. Seroquel makes me twitch involuntarily. If this persists, it will be called Tardive Dyskinesia, the condition that makes Seroquel dangerous. For now, a twitching body is better than a dead body.

If you are reading this and unsure about medication, here is a summary of my feelings after a ten year wrestling match against the idea of medication: Medication can do wonders, but it's not a cure all. No one would subject herself to radiation or chemotherapy unless she knew it was her best chance of getting back to "normal." But to those with cancer, these two treatments are worth it. Mental illnesses are similar, and I think anti-depressants are probably way over-prescribed. A lot of people probably just need an extra hug, a good cup of coffee, or a talk therapist. But if your life is being hindered by anxiety, mood swings, depression, etc. on a daily basis, find the right psychiatrist – one who listens and cares – and get over the stigma of medication. Who cares what someone else thinks? (Well, I do for one!) But you shouldn't care. It's your life and your body, and you know what you feel. Be your own advocate, and go find a drug that helps. Be careful of cure-alls (my Vyvanse experience) because they can set you back years. Trust the medication about which you think this: "Well, it surely isn't perfect, but I prefer this particular struggle over the one I'm trying to cure."

Chapter 7: The Sanest Place on Earth

At age 35, I finally found a semblance of sanity, thanks to Dr. Zhang and medication. But 35 years of insanity has taken a toll – on me, on my family, on my wife, on my children. As I've processed what I've been through to finally reach a place where I feel like I can process things without fear being the motor that turns the wheel in my head, I've become angry. Primarily, I am angry that it's so hard to find places where we can share our real burdens with others.

In II Corinthians 12:10, Paul says he has come to boast in his weaknesses, for those are the places where God shines through him. But even in church, we aren't allowed to be weak. Churches are some of the most façade-laden places I've encountered. And if we are going to be weak in church, it needs to fall within a specific list of acceptable struggles: alcohol is okay unless you belong to a denomination that denounces all drinking; lust is okay as long as you're a run-of-the-mill, heterosexual luster; family troubles are okay as long as divorce isn't something you're considering.

But mental illness is not exactly acceptable in many church circles. Many still tell one to "pray away" their struggles, believing that any mental struggle must actually be a

spiritual battle – a lack of faith or even demonic influence.
Nor is homosexuality. Try telling most people in church that
you struggle with attraction to the same sex, and you will get
the same reaction as they'll give you for mental illness:
"That's a spiritual problem; we can pray that away. We can
lay hands on you and you will be healed. It's just something
from your upbringing that needs to be dealt with. Jesus will
fix you." Nor is questioning the traditional, conservative
views of Christianity – questions like whether hell exists (see
Appendix regarding this question), whether or not God really
is good when all this evil exists, etc. Nor are a myriad of
other common struggles and questions.

Ironically, my three days in hell (the mental hospital) were
the closest I've come to finding the sort of heavenly
ragamuffin community I've always longed for. Somehow,
despite being essentially imprisoned; despite being
surrounded by strangers; despite being petrified that I would
never again be without this consuming depression…despite
all of that, I now look back on those days with fondness.
Though I have no contact with the people I met "in there," I
feel a deep bond with them, and I hope I will get to reunite
with them someday. There were black people, white people,
poor people, rich people, smart people, not-so-smart people,
drug addicts, sober people…and all of us came together in
the hospital as a community – a "confederacy of dunces," to
quote the book title.

But I think that's what Jesus wants us to be! That's when he
makes the most use of us – when we quit pretending to be

something we're not and start "making our mess our message," as Robin Roberts recently said of her battle with a rare bone marrow disease. The mess ain't going anywhere, and if this life is all there is, then I'm all for hedonism, frankly. But if there's more, then we have hope, and we can start being honest in the midst of our mess, sharing our struggles with others, entering into others' struggles with them, bearing one another's burdens, and ushering in the kingdom of God on earth.

Let me tell you a little bit about the saints I met in the hospital:

My roommate was a man I'll call Brett. Brett looked a lot like me – white, clean cut, dashingly handsome (like me, I said). Brett was there voluntarily to receive ECT – what we used to call "shock therapy." He had struggled with intense depression, and ECT was his last resort to get his brain to rewire. He was divorced and had two kids. His relationship with his ex-wife was acrimonious. He chose to come to the hospital as an inpatient "because [he] didn't really have a support network on the outside." Given that Brett was a Christian and a church-goer, I find this remarkably sad. How can the church claim to be anything other than a social club when a man like this can sit in its pews week in and week out without developing a support network to surround him? Maybe it was his own fault for not reaching out, but at least part of the blame belongs on the shoulders of all of us who have allowed church to be a place where façades are firmly fixed in place, where we don't let others see us sweat, where we pretend that our "salvation" has made us whole rather than being necessary because of how completely fucked up we really are. I'm in favor of a church full of fuck-ups.

I got to know another man named Carl. When visitation hours were approaching, I asked him if anyone was coming to see him. "Me? Hell no. I live an hour and a half from here. No one cares enough about me to drive that far!" Since he knew I was having visitors, he did ask if I knew anyone who could bring him a pack of Marlboros, and I happily complied by asking my wife to bring them. He nearly teared up when I gave him the pack of cigarettes later that evening, and he offered to pay me back when he got out. I refused, and he didn't seem to know how to thank me for this small gesture of kindness. Somehow, I'm pretty sure Jesus would've bought the guy cigarettes, too...and maybe even smoked a few with him. Carl came from the opposite side of the tracks, to say the least. But in the hospital, we were comrades, brothers, equals...just two guys fighting for sanity amidst some painful mental illnesses.

The man I worried most about from my time in the hospital was a man named John. He was only there for one day. His insurance company wouldn't let him stay. He had driven himself to the hospital, knowing that he was on the brink of suicide. He was terrified of being sent home, but he had no choice. I often wonder what became of him.

Then there was Steve. Steve probably weighed 400 pounds. In one of our group sessions, they had us go around and tell about something that made us hopeful, something that we should fight for. Steve shared something he had already shared with me in a different setting: He adored his wife and five children. He wanted to grow old with his wife and to walk his little girls down the aisle. He wanted to be there for his kids. Not exactly a unique wish, but his depression had made it hard for him to keep pressing on. He was no stranger to mental hospitals; he was the one who offered me a systematic breakdown of why the hospital across town was much better than this particular one. I could see the ache in his eyes. He wanted to be able to work and contribute to his family's well-being, but his depression was too crippling.

Dean was probably the most "like me" of anyone I met in the hospital. He was as wide-eyed as I was, completely shocked and overwhelmed to be where he was. Unlike most of the others, Dean and I were first-timers. He spent a lot of time the first evening trying to convince those of us who would listen that he had things together: "I drive a convertible. I'm Mr. Outgoing! I am usually the fun one. I don't know what's happened to me!" It's called bi-polar, Dean, we told him. Dean would skip out on the morning meetings, too depressed to get out of bed. By evening, he would hang out with the rest of us, seeming 100% "normal." On visitation night, he asked his dad, who had come from Miami to be near his son in this trying time, not to come. Dean didn't feel like seeing anyone. Thankfully, mercifully, his dad and a female friend showed up anyway. In the end, Dean was glad they came, just as most of us want the comfort of others when we are at our worst, even though we may not want them to see us "like that" initially.

Finally, a man named Keith accompanied me to my first (and only) AA meeting. Anyone was welcome to go, and it was a chance to get off of the locked hall, so I decided to give it a try. Many people have marveled at the success of AA, and I think its success is rather simple: it's a community of screwed up people being honest about their struggles. If every one of us could join a similar community and attend a meeting regularly where we shared our deepest struggles, longings, and weaknesses, I think we'd be a lot healthier as a society. I didn't get to know Keith, but to this day, he still has one of my favorite long-sleeve t-shirts. He had nothing to keep him warm, and that place was freezing (perhaps cold people are less likely to kill themselves?!). When I was leaving, he asked if he could keep the shirt. I've certainly read the Bible enough times to know what I'm supposed to do when someone asks for my shirt, so I let him keep it, but I wasn't quite as thrilled about it as I was probably supposed to be. I failed to also offer him my tunic.

***

In the hospital, at my lowest moment, I found authentic community. Sadly, I have yet to find it outside of the hospital, and I certainly haven't found it in any church. The verse from Corinthians that I referred to at the beginning of this chapter illustrates exactly what I'm getting at through these stories: We are all weak, but when we embrace that weakness and open it up honestly to others, somehow, some way, God takes it and makes it something beautiful, even powerful. But it starts with our willingness to lay bare our wounds and let others help us deal with them. God's power is found in weakness and in the community that can (but rarely does) spring up from weakness.

Henri Nouwen, a deceased Catholic priest who struggled with intense loneliness throughout his life, says it this way: "A Christian community is therefore a healing community not because wounds and pains are alleviated, but because wounds and pains become openings or occasions for a new vision. Mutual confession then becomes a mutual deepening of hope, and sharing of weakness becomes a reminder to one and all of the coming strength." Incidentally, Nouwen was a closet, celibate homosexual who refused to share his burden with anyone other than a select few for fear of what the revelation would do to his ministry. What a shame that a man who was as committed to the ways of Jesus as just about anyone could possibly be didn't feel comfortable standing in front of the church and saying, "I am wrestling with homosexuality. I don't want to act on it, but it's my strongest temptation." If I can find a church where one is open to express such a struggle, I'll be joining it. That will be the authentic Church – a place where we can all be screwed up together, collectively hoping in the promises of salvation.

***

Oddly, I love hospitals, so long as I'm not a patient in one. In the hospital, people are raw and real; people lose their façades. Same thing with AA meetings. I'm thinking of becoming an alcoholic just so I can share in that brotherhood. Façades are the ultimate representation of our brokenness, our shame. Every morning, as we're getting dressed, we are literally getting into costume, dressing the part of the person we want others to think we are. Through the day, we practice our act; we try to stay in character as best as possible.

A recent encounter illustrates this point well: A friend came to me to ask for a copy of a devotional I had given publicly. He ended up crying and sharing with me that his son had "done something stupid" and gotten himself in some legal trouble. He was embarrassed to be crying and, though he never told me what his son had done, he did say, mainly to himself, "If word of what he did ever got out, it would be *awful.*" That was the end of his explanation, but he was clearly mortified by what his son had done. And even more mortified by the thought of others knowing that his son had screwed up.

I was sad for him – about his son, yes, but even more so that he was so married to his façade that he couldn't bear the thought of being "outed" as the father of a boy who screwed up. Yet from my vantage point, there's almost nothing he could've done that would make me reject my friend. People do really, really dumb stuff. I mean REALLY DUMB. But if he were willing to share it with others, as Nouwen says, his vulnerability and honesty and rawness could become a soft place for others who struggle to land.

Even Jesus chose weakness as a way to change the world. He submitted to death at the hands of people who wrongly accused him. He was spat on and whipped only one week after being worshipped as he rode into Jerusalem on a donkey. He chose to be born to a nameless couple, to work as a carpenter rather than as a king. He chose weakness because, somehow, through weakness God's power can show up best.

I think God's promises for healing will look a lot different than we think they will. My homosexual friend who first introduced me to the idea of medication has prayed for healing from his homosexuality. He's been anointed with oil and had hands laid on him. Guess what…he's still attracted to men. But through his homosexuality, I think God has deepened his capacity for compassion. He's one of the most tender-hearted people I know. He's a great friend, too. But I don't think he'd have these capacities without his "brokenness."

And I think it was the same with Henri Nouwen. His closet homosexuality enabled him to write about the very deepest sort of loneliness, and through his words, countless people have realized that they are not quite as alone as they had thought. Others can relate.

***

The other day I went bowling, and at the other end of the facility was a large group of mentally handicapped people. In the bathroom, I encountered one of them who, without prompting, started telling me about how bad of a day he was having because a girl had dumped him, and one of his friends had been mean to him. As best I could, I tried to offer compassion, but I walked away wishing it was that easy for those of us who are "normal" to share our burdens with others – we'd all be a lot more sane.

I've spent my entire 36 years battling OCD and anxiety, trying to keep up the façade that I'm put-together. Recently, I went to tutor at a Boys and Girls' Club, and a girl told me I "looked rich." Amused, but also curious, I asked her what made me look rich. She didn't quite know how to answer this question and said, "Your face and your clothes." While it was a funny moment, it was also telling. I guess I'm doing too good of a job with this façade thing. I know how to dress the part of the rich, put-together white guy. I'm working hard to take the mask off, but society isn't always ready for realness. Society is one big costume party where most of us simply find a costume that suits us well and wear it proudly until our dying day. We'll never fix that problem entirely, but when the church becomes willing to be a place where costumes can be left at the door, I feel certain that it will become the place of hope and healing that it was intended to be. For now, it's really no different than a social club where people who like to wear similar costumes go once a week to hear someone give a talk who also wears a similar costume. Sadly, the mental hospital was the best church I've ever been to. I can't find one nearly as compelling now that I'm back in the world of "sane" people.

Chapter 8: To Be Continued

I'm only 36-year-old as I write this. I have only known I have a mental illness for the past 11 years. I have only admitted that I have OCD for the past 5 or 6 years. I have only surrendered to my need for medication over the past 2 years. I have only realized the presence of God's love over the past few months.

I have a long way to go. And I am way less sure of what lays ahead than I was when my adult life began. I am way less sure of what it means to be a Christian than I used to be.

But I'm learning to be okay with uncertainty. I'm learning to be okay with the fact that others will disagree with me about many facets of this book. That's fine. This book isn't for them anyway.

This book is intended to be an encouragement to anyone who has battled mental illness, religious dogmatism, or both. Be bold, my friends. Share your struggles with other people. They might need a soft place to land with their own battles. You might make some of the truest friends you will ever have. At worst, they'll think you're crazy, but in my case, I tend to agree with them – I am crazy. So at least now we have a starting point to agree on. Let's talk. Let's be crazy together. That's what Jesus wanted.

So, please, do the world a huge favor: share your story.

Make your mess your message.

Appendix: The Ultimate Uncertainty: What Happens When I Die?

As I have mentioned many times throughout this memoir, the most overwhelming uncertainty in my mind comes from the question of hell. Quite simply, if God loves me so much to die for me, how can he also allow people to suffer eternally in hell? The incongruity of these two concepts has plagued my brain in ways both obvious and not-so-obvious. It's a question well worth addressing at some length.

OCD thrives on the uncertainties in life – how can I be sure I've washed all the germs off my hands? How can I be sure my parents won't abandon me? How can I be sure I am "saved" and will go to heaven? How can I be sure I'm in the right relationship? These are the questions that have never been far from my brain throughout my life.

Religion, on the other hand, attempts to provide certainty about things which are very much uncertain. How was the earth created? What is humanity's purpose? Where are the lines between right and wrong? What happens to people when they die? These are tough questions, but religion provides explanations. In other words, religion attempts to provide certainty where there is none.

In my world, I had two very strong warriors waging a constant battle for my brain, especially when it came to the ultimate uncertainty: what happens when we die. As I've said, my middle school years were consumed by this particular question, but in a broader sense, I think the central question in my mind has always been about how I can know that God is actually a good guy and that he loves me. All of my obsessions have come back to the central uncertainty of how to achieve peace...how to know that *things* would turn out to be okay.

At the center of these forms of uncertainty is the question of hell. In my case, how could I be sure I wouldn't end up there? In a global sense, how could a good God actually allow such a place to exist, or even create such a place?

I'm well aware of all the normal Christian answers. Here's a sampling of some popular ones:

- God doesn't send people to hell; people's sin sends them to hell.
- God's wrath at our sin has to be satisfied. For Christians, Jesus satisfies that wrath. For non-Christians, eternal damnation satisfies that wrath.
- God's ways are higher than our ways. We can't understand him, but we can be certain that he is good, and thus, if he invented/allows there to be a hell, it must be in line with his good character.

Over the course of my adult life, I had gradually grown to have a notion of hell that is different from the traditional views of people burning eternally, but I hadn't really solidified my perspective until last summer, when three of our friends died unexpectedly at different times. Though I had quit believing that hell was a literal place of "fire and brimstone," I still had a latent fear that God wasn't really good, that he couldn't really be trusted if hell existed at all. I was still scared of God more than any other emotion.

Attending 3 unexpected funerals, all of which were for people under the age of 40, will make one do some thinking about what comes after this life. One of the funerals was for a six and a half year old girl with a chronic illness. Next was a friend's sister who died mysteriously in her sleep. The final one was for 37-year-old father of four small children. He dropped dead out of nowhere.

In the aftermath of all of these deaths, people said what they always say: "She's in a better place now, no more suffering for her." Or, "One day you'll all be together in heaven forever!" But just because I'm on medication doesn't mean I'm not still really good at asking what if questions, and every time I heard someone offer the bereaved a trite bit of encouragement, I thought to myself, "How can you possibly know that?! What if he/she is in hell?!!! What if you'll never see him/her again? What if the only way you can hope to see him/her again is if you, too, join the eternal torment of the unsaved? What if the difficulty of the life he/she left is nothing compared to the torture he/she is in now…forever…with zero hope for relief?"

It was time to ask the question I had always "known" the answer to: What really happens when people die? My underlying assumption had always been rather simple: "unsaved" people go to hell. The "saved" (this was a slippery concept, yes, but it involved "knowing" Jesus as one's personal savior) go to heaven.

***

It's easy to have theories about death and the afterlife when death is removed and impersonal, but when it hits close to home, the questions suddenly need satisfying answers, not spiritual platitudes. I was hit hard by these deaths. I couldn't help but imagine holding my little girl's dead body as I had watched our friends do for their daughter. I couldn't help but imagine being the dead father of young children, wondering how my absence would impact my kids' lives. I was sinking into despair as the need for clarity about the afterlife grew more and more palpable. Frankly, I was ready to give up on virtually everything I had ever believed, but the other alternatives seemed horrendous: I could believe that there was no such thing as a God and that I would simply die and rot in the ground. Or I could believe in a God who chose between the good people and the bad people, who saved some and damned others. Neither of these options offered me any comfort whatsoever. I couldn't see any hopeful way forward.

Despondent, I decided it was time to research the question of hell and face my fear that God might actually be a sadistic torturer. I didn't have to look far before realizing that there are plenty of alternative Christian opinions to the ones that had terrified me throughout my life. Without even trying very hard, I found countless opinions that offered more hopeful interpretations of the Bible than what I had known all my life. At first I was skeptical, convinced that these people certainly were overlooking the truth. Gradually, I realized that there really is (lots of) evidence that will enable one to quit believing in the concept of eternal damnation.

What follows is what I have found in my research, and though I will never quit asking what if questions, these discoveries have provided great relief for my obsessive fear of God.

***

To begin with and most importantly, the notion of hell as a place of eternal torture/suffering is simply not in the Bible. The word "hell" came from translators' desires to simplify the various words and concepts surrounding the afterlife. Neither the word nor the current concept of hell appears anywhere in the Bible. The concept of hell only exists because fear is a powerful motivator, but the choice to translate many words that referred to the next life into one simple word, hell, was a radical leap based on what the original manuscripts actually said. There are four words in the original manuscripts which all have come to be translated "hell." They are Sheol, Hades, Tartarus, and Gehenna. The first three all meant "the land of the unseen," and many righteous people throughout the Bible were described as being in that very land. Keep reading for a discussion of "Gehenna," the term Jesus seemed most fond of.

Next, The Old Testament never mentions hell. The "wrathful" God who seemed to pick favorites and destroy entire populations never threatens people with hell. When Adam and Eve sinned, the punishment was DEATH, not hell. When God wiped out the world with the flood, he said nothing about eternal damnation. Nothing. He killed a bunch of people, yes, but he didn't then make sure they kept on suffering. If anything, he acted in mercy because they had become so despicable (according the Biblical account). Sin makes people horribly unhappy, even if they think they are happy. Alcoholics, drug addicts, or even your run-of-the-mill sinners may well think they are happy in the moment of sin, but sin leads to misery every single time. So, God, in his mercy, destroyed the world that was full of sin. Don't you think it's suspicious that he did this without mentioning to people or without having Noah mention to people that they were in danger of hell? They were in danger of *death*, not hell.

Third, death as the punishment for sin is consistent with the character of a merciful God. After all, who would want to live forever on this planet? Life is hard, that's why there are lots of bitter people. Death is a tough thing to deal with, but not as tough as having to live long enough to see the world continue to crumble around you. I'm grateful that I will die someday. I'm also grateful that people like Hitler eventually die. Romans 6:23 says, "The wages of sin is *death*," not hell. The wages of sin being death makes logical sense. The idea of God allowing or causing people to be eternally kept alive so they could experience torture makes no sense. Not even Hitler tortured the Jews unceasingly. He was more concerned with annihilating them than torturing them (though plenty of torture was involved, for sure). So, if there is such a thing as *eternal* torture, God is the worst tyrant in the history of the world for allowing such a place to exist when he could put a stop to it. How can we attribute to God a characteristic that we don't even attribute to Hitler or bin Laden? Wouldn't God be kind enough to at least put us out of our sinful misery?

Fourth, and this is where I began to find myself won over to a new way of seeing eternity, Paul never mentions hell. Paul...the first theologian! The guy who gave the Reformed folks their pet verses about predestination (God picks his favorites for salvation and discards the rest into hell) never mentions hell. Not once. The guy who explained what Jesus was all about to everyone from Augustine to my five-year-old forgot to mention hell. Uh, Paul, that would be a rather important thing to talk about, my friend. Perhaps we just lost that book somewhere along the way. But look it up. He says nothing.

And guess who else never mentions it...Jesus. "Whoa, now," you're saying, "I can show you where he mentions it." But he didn't. Every time Jesus referred to hell, he used the word "Gehenna" or "Hades." Gehenna was a reference to a literal trash dump outside of Jerusalem. He only refers to it in a very few places – 5 times in the synoptic (combined) gospels by my count. And every single time it's used, it is directed at the Jews of the day, most likely as a prophecy that, unless they changed courses, they would quite literally be thrown into the trash dump of Gehenna – this is exactly where the Romans threw Jewish bodies when they invaded Jerusalem shortly after Jesus's death. As for Hades, that simply meant "the land of the dead" at the time – a vague concept with no particular implications about eternal punishment. Was Jesus being metaphorical when he mentioned Gehenna and Hades? Possibly. But not for a place of eternal torture. If you threatened to throw people in the trash, you wouldn't be threatening them with eternal suffering. You'd be saying, "Be careful that the eye that's causing you to sin doesn't cause your whole being to become so sin-filled that you need to be thrown out, burned up, as we burn up trash." When you burn useless things, you don't make sure they are feeling the full effects of the fire you've thrown them in. You just can't use them and you need them to be destroyed, not tortured.

Even when Jesus refers to an "eternal *punishment*" in places like Matthew 25:46, that does not remotely have to mean eternal *suffering*. If I cut off my finger because it is causing me to sin, that punishment will last for my entire life. It is a life-long punishment, but the pain of the first few minutes won't last my whole life. Eventually, the pain will subside and I will learn to live without the finger. The punishment lasts, but not the pain. Not even the worst tyrant in the history of the world...not even a pimp who sells sex slaves to disgusting men...not Adolf Hitler or Mao Zedong tortured people incessantly. To characterize God as someone who would see it as warranted to make people suffer eternally is to characterize him as a monster unlike any the world has ever seen. No wonder we are sheepish when we talk about this particular concept of hell. We should be!

Finally, pure logic says that the traditional Christian ideas about hell make no sense at all. Here's the essence of our story: The God of the Old Testament (who never threatens anyone with hell) sends his son, Jesus, to be the savior of all mankind. But with a rather large catch: He's only the savior of those who "accept him" (who knows exactly what that means? Do I say a prayer? Bear enough "fruit"?). Those who don't accept him suffer eternally in a fiery pit, being kept alive by God in the midst of the flames for the purpose of unquenchable suffering. They didn't get the prayer worded quite right, didn't have quite the right understanding of Jesus. No one ever wandered past their neck of the woods to set them straight with a Christian tract or the Sinner's Prayer. They had just passed the "age of accountability" as a young adult but were a little less mature than others in their philosophical thinking and they hadn't gotten around to pondering their eternal destination just yet. They passionately sought God and truth, but believed in Mohammed or Buddha or Krishna as being a little too important. Poor, doomed unbelievers! This concept is simply illogical, and God would want us to use our logic when interpreting the confusing things he says. "God loves all of us as his own children" and "God will send unrepentant sinners to a place of eternal fiery torture" are mutually exclusive. They simply can't both be true.

***

As I began to ponder these new possibilities about God's character, my fear of him began to diminish. My whole life has been one big obsessive fear of screwing up – screwing up this life and ruining the potential joys it has to offer, and screwing up my eternal fate or others' eternal fate through my actions/inactions. I began to realize that it might actually be possible to trust God as the "loving" God so many claimed he was/is. I have always been able to explain away other troubling attributes of God (for a different book, I suppose), but the traditional notion of hell has always been inexplicable to me.

Honestly, I don't think most Christians genuinely believe in the traditional concept either. I think most sort of think they are supposed to believe in a place of eternal torture, but would prefer to focus on other aspects of Christianity because the notion of people being tortured forever is so hard to defend. If we really believe in a place where people suffer forever with no chance of escape, we really shouldn't talk about anything else...ever!

Here's what I mean: Imagine that you went to a mall and while eating in the food court recognized a child molester from your see-if-a-child-molester-lives-next-door app (these really exist). Imagine that this guy was no ordinary child molester, but one of America's Most Wanted child molesters. You see him head into the bathroom where he is known to prey on unsuspecting children. You stand outside the bathroom, not quite sure what to do, how to tell people he's in there without seeming like a lunatic yourself. As the first small child wanders toward the bathroom, you wouldn't use the tactics that most Christians use to try to convert people – try to befriend the kid, get to know him better, gain his trust, and then, when the time is right, you'll tell him the news that he might want to choose a different bathroom. Problem is, he has to pee, and he's been told not to talk to strangers, and he politely ignores you and walks on by.

What would you do next?

You'd grab the kid and yell, right?! You don't care if his mother gets the terrifying mall cops involved, or even the real cops. You can explain yourself later. In the meantime, you just saved him from being sodomized.

Here's my point: If people really believed in hell, they wouldn't care if people thought they were the nuttiest of the nutty. They'd tell every single person they met. They'd put crazy messages on their car, not caring who honked at them for being a nut-job. They'd join the guy on the street corner, preaching to anyone who would listen. They'd quit their jobs and go into full-time ministry, telling every single person they could find that if they were in a car accident on the way home and they hadn't repented, they would be eternally screwed – tortured without any hope of ever escaping.

But very few do that, either because they aren't so sure about hell or because they're rather selfish. I think most are less certain that hell is a real place than they are willing to admit.

***

For the person whose mental illnesses are inextricably enmeshed with his religious views, resolving the question of hell can be a major step forward. It has been for me. OCD is ultimately based in the fear of the "what if?!" What if I told a lie? What if I'm not really saved? What if I die because I didn't get my hands clean enough? What if I kill someone else accidentally? All of these questions are more than a little daunting if we can't be sure that God really cares about our well-being. If God is a monster who is looking for a reason to spank his children, then there's a lot to be afraid of.

My whole life, this has been the crux of my fear – that I might actually be wrong about something as important as who I marry or where I will spend eternity, that God is actually only loving to those who "get it right," to those who are "chosen" or "saved." Yet inside my rapid-fire brain, I've never been able to be certain what this mysterious salvation actually looks or feels like. I've never attained any certainty that God actually loves and forgives me.

And think what you will, but I believe that God, in his mercy, was ready to help me take a huge step forward as he

has led me to realize the truth that hell is a man-made concept, not a God-made one. Hell had been a stumbling block for me all my life…how could I possibly know that God loved me? How could I possibly know that God was in fact a loving entity if he was sending people to eternal doom? This was not a God I could trust, even if I myself was saved. This was a God to be feared, a God who let babies go to hell, a God who sent devout Buddhists, who had spent their lives pursuing him, to hell to suffer with the burning babies. A God who would let Jeffrey Dahmer, who accepted Christ in prison, into heaven but would send Gandhi to hell. Man, it's hard to understand this mysteriously loving/spiteful God! Sure hope I have it right. Sure hope I have it right. Sure hope I have it right. Sure hope I have it right. Sure hope I have it right. Sure hope I have it right. Sure hope I have it right. Sure hope I have it right. Sure hope I have it right.
Sure hope I have it right. Sure hope I have it right. Sure hope I have it right. Sure hope I have it right. Sure hope I have it right. Sure hope I have it right. Sure hope I have it right.
Sure hope I have it right. Sure hope I have it right. Sure hope I have it right. Sure hope I have it right. Sure hope I have it right. Sure hope I have it right. Sure hope I have it right.
Sure hope I have it right. Sure hope I have it right. Sure hope I have it right. Sure hope I have it right. Sure hope I have it right. Sure hope I have it right. Sure hope I have it right.
Sure hope I have it right. Sure hope I have it right. Sure hope I have it right. Sure hope I have it right. Sure hope I have it right. Sure hope I have it right. Sure hope I have it right.
Sure hope I have it right. Sure hope I have it right. Sure hope

I have it right. Sure hope I have it right. Sure hope I have it right. Sure hope I have it right. Sure hope I have it right. Sure hope I have it right. Sure hope I have it right. Sure hope I have it right. Sure hope I have it right. Sure hope I have it right. Sure hope I have it right. Sure hope I have it right. Sure hope I have it right. Sure hope I have it right. Sure hope I have it right. Sure hope I have it right.

But if hell is a myth perpetrated by humans as a fear tactic, I can finally believe that God really is loving. God will love me if my marriage falls apart. God will still love me if I commit an accidental sin (or a zillion). God will love me if I am gay or struggle with alcohol abuse or start selling drugs.

Jesus warned me about sin *because sin is bad for ME*, not because sin will doom me to hell for eternity. From the beginning of time, God's warnings about our behavior have simply been his way of saying, "Look, I designed you, and I know what's best for you. Faithfulness to your spouse is better than a sexual free-for-all (just look at Tiger Woods's as exhibit A on that one). Telling the truth is ultimately better than lying, even though lying seems expedient at the time. Loving me and following me will ultimately lead you to the happiness/joy you are seeking in drugs, alcohol, and sex. Loving other people, though difficult, will ultimately fulfill you far more than living selfishly will. Keeping a day of rest set aside is something you need deep within you; following the busyness of your culture will wear you down and keep you from the good things I've intended..."

God's words to us are full of mercy! And not just for those of us who have our "get out of hell" cards in our pockets. The good news we are to spread is quite simple: God loves you! And he wants better things for you than you want for yourself. Follow God's ways and you will grow in joy and peace and kindness. Keep following your own ways and you'll become more and more miserable until you are relieved from misery by death – God's merciful gift.

***

So what happens to non-followers after death? I don't really have a clue, but right after Paul says the wages of sin is death in Romans 6:23, he contrasts it by saying, "The free gift of God in Jesus Christ is eternal life." Eternal life wouldn't be much of a gift if many people spent it in hell. The reality is, there are a lot of confusing verses in the Bible, and our "pet" interpretations of them offer Pharisaical interpretations rather than acknowledging that some verses raise legitimately confusing questions that we just can't answer from our vantage point.

Here's another challenging verse for our hellish notions: "Every knee will bow before me; every tongue will acknowledge God" (Romans 14:11). I don't pretend to know exactly how that works or if everyone ends up in heaven. But I have come to feel quite secure in believing that God really is the Good Guy who's looking out for everyone. Maybe he'll just destroy those who don't want anything to do with him, or maybe they, too, will see the light somehow in the next life. Who knows? Not me.

But in my battle against whatever mixture of mental illnesses I have, my life has been radically changed by this freeing reality. Life is still hard. I still have OCD, anxiety, depression, and bi-polar disorder (maybe). And these still cause me and my loved ones plenty of pain. As I said at the beginning, it's a chemical problem, not a spiritual one, and I, for one, haven't gotten my miracle just yet.

***

Or maybe I have a million every-day miracles:

Maybe Ann's patience and our ever-strengthening marriage is a miracle.

Maybe finding Dr. Zhang is a miracle.

Maybe my friendship with Walter is miraculous.

Maybe my friendship with Tim, who also has OCD, is a miracle.

Maybe my friend and mentor, Mike, who sees God differently than anyone else I know, is a miracle in my life as he allows me to question God, to be angry at God, and to come to new views of who God is.

Maybe having the support of faithful friends like Brad, Michael, Andrew, Frank, Glenn, and Steve is a miracle.

***

Still, I'm not "cured." My brain still tortures me in ways that I think sadistic torturers and murderers might enjoy learning how to inflict on others. But I have never felt so light in my spirit as I have since I realized that I can stand on very solid footing and believe that God is indeed loving, not a sadistic, arbitrary torturer.

Now God seems merciful, even as he refines me and disciplines me. Now God seems ultimately kind, even as the world inside my head remains very unkind at times. Now God seems loving, even as I struggle so desperately to love those around me. Now God seems gentle, even as horrible things like premature deaths continue to happen. This is a God I can cling to.

References

Chapter 1

Psalm 23:1, NIV: "The Lord is my Shepherd; I shall not be in want."

Chapter 2

1 John 4:18, NKJV: 'Perfect love casts out fear.'"

John 16:33, NIV: "In this world you will have trouble. But take heart! I have overcome the world."

Chapter 3

Hebrews 10:26, NLT: "Dear friends, if we deliberately continue sinning after we have received knowledge of the truth, there is no longer any sacrifice that will cover these sins."

Chapter 5

Kay, D.M. *Sleeping with ROCD: Power for the Co-Sufferers of Relationship OCD*. http://www.sleeping-with-rocd.com/

Matthew 7:7, NIV: "Ask and it will be given to you; seek and you will find; knock and the door will be opened to you."

Hebrews 12:6, NIV: "because the Lord disciplines the one he loves, and he chastens everyone he accepts as his son."

Chapter 6

Ephesians 5:25, NIV: "Husbands, love your wives, just as Christ loved the church and gave himself up for her."

Mark 5:1-20: Jesus casts demons into a herd of pigs.

Chapter 7

2 Corinthians 12:10, NIV: "That is why, for Christ's sake, I delight in weaknesses, in insults, in hardships, in persecutions, in difficulties. For when I am weak, then I am strong."

Toole, John Kennedy. *A Confederacy of Dunces*. New York: Grove Press, 1980.

Luke 6:29, NIV: "If someone takes your cloak, do not stop him from taking your tunic."

Nouwen, Henri. *The Wounded Healer*. New York: Doubleday, 1972.

Appendix

Romans 6:23, NIV: "For the wages of sin is death, but the gift of God is eternal life in[a] Christ Jesus our Lord."

Matthew 25:46, NIV: "Then they will go away to eternal punishment, but the righteous to eternal life."

Romans 14:11, NIV: "'As surely as I live,' says the Lord, 'every knee will bow before me; every tongue will acknowledge God.'" (Jesus is quoting Isaiah 45:23).

Acknowledgements

First and foremost, thanks to my wife, Ann, both for putting up with my OCD and for helping/allowing me to tell this story as candidly as I have. You're just right for me, my love, and you're beautiful, inside and out. Thanks to my kids for their patience with daddy as he works through his difficulties with his brain in the midst of the chaos of having little people around. I adore you guys. Thanks to my mom and dad for their receptivity to this story. I am profoundly grateful to have you guys as parents and partners in this life. Thanks to my siblings for their encouragement and support in both the tough moments and the ones that are just plain fun. You guys make life even more worth living. Thanks to the friends I mention throughout this book. Your support and kindness is why I'm still here. And thanks to God for helping me to make this mess part of his message. You are a mystery to me, but I'm working on letting you love me.

About the Author

Tim Blue is a husband to Ann, a father to the two most precious children on earth, an English teacher and department chair, a respectable golfer, a very inconsistent and reluctant exerciser, a diet Coke addict, a filter-less joke teller, a tormented soul, a skeptical Christian, and a lot of other things I shouldn't put in print here.

Contact: I would love to hear from you. Email me at timronblue@yahoo.com any time.

Blog: http://timronblue.wordpress.com

Made in the USA
Charleston, SC
11 December 2012